Benjamín Collado Hinarejos

Sex and Erotism in Ancient Egypt

Benjamín Collado Hinarejos

ISBN-13: 978-1539170549

ISBN-10: 1539170543

Cover: erotic papyrus of Turin. Modified by author

Terracotta group dated from Ptolemaic era showing a couple in the sexual act, accompanied by other individuals represented in a smaller size. Note that the male protagonist, apart from having a huge member, has the side ponytail that in ancient Egypt identified children. (New York) Brooklyn Museum.

About the Author

My love for history and archeology have accompanied me since childhood, and I've been fortunate to grow up in an area rich in remains from various past cultures; something that has given me the opportunity to participate in numerous archaeological excavations in ruins of the Iberian and Roman period in Spain. I graduated in History, specializing in Ancient History and Protohistory, and so far I have published the books "The Iberians" -Spanish- (Akal, 2013), "The Iberians and their World" -Spanish- (Akal, 2014), "The Iberians and the War" -Spanish- (Amazon, 2014), "Tutankhamun's Tomb and the Curse of the Mummies" - English - (Amazon, 2016), "The Royal Mummies' Hideout" -English- (Amazon, 2015), "The Silver Pharaohs" -English- (Amazon, 2016), and the one you have in your hands.

Table of Content

1.- Music scene with dancers detail, painted on the walls of the tomb of Nebamun at Thebes (S. XIV B.C.). Images full of sensuality like this have permeated the popular imagination. British Museum in London.

1.- Introduction

What ideas do we have of eroticism in ancient Egypt? Surely most people whom we might ask this question would say that the first thing that comes into their heads is the image of scantily dressed dancers, twisting lewdly before the pharaoh who, pleased, watches the show from his throne as young maids, half his age, serve him wine naked, or just covering themselves with some transparencies.

These images are certainly real as they are widely represented in Egyptian art. But a lot of tendentious information was added by other ancient, mostly Roman sources, and has entered our collective imaginations. Stories like those tales of the "depraved" Cleopatra, the queen that shocked Rome by seducing some of its most illustrious sons (Julius Caesar and Mark Antony), whose sex lives people then took the time to air and amplify to absurdity. This is likely why an idea permeated in popular imagination of a sexually uninhibited Egypt, if not perverted and degenerate, where all possible sexual behaviors, including those considered more reprehensible, took place.

The truth is that, beyond these apparent exaggerations and distortions, we are faced with a paradox that despite being a culture where sexuality was seen more naturally and freely than in other ancient peoples such as the Greeks or Romans, there are barely any examples of erotic art or explicit mentions of the sexual practice beyond that which developed between their gods; quite the opposite of the other two aforementioned cultures where we find numerous written stories of openly erotic subject and sexual representations in paintings, sculptures, jewelry etc.

Yet the evidence suggests that in ancient Egypt sex in general was seen as an open activity, far from the negative connotations and feelings of guilt that we see in other cultures, both ancient and current. But we can't forget that the Egyptian culture developed over more than 3,000 years, and it's very likely that during that vast period of time, the views on sexuality and eroticism were changing and going through periods of more or less freedom and permissiveness as trends. This is something that has been seen on many occasions, for example in the decoration of a tomb of the XVIII Dynasty, where a naked maid was originally painted, but several decades later the new owner felt that the image was not appropriate and had it retouched by adding clothes that would cover her body. This is just a sample and could simply be a matter of personal taste, but it is not the only sign.

Both in paintings and reliefs of the tombs and monuments, as well as in some papyruses, it is relatively common to find scenes with men and women totally naked or barely covered; something that has contributed to the image of a society steeped in eroticism and sensuality. But even though some current authors have insisted on the idea that perhaps for Egyptians these images may not have the same erotic implications we perceive, the references found in various texts, especially in the love poetry of the Ramesside times, we find the opposite. For them, the half-naked bodies, the exposed breasts and transparent dresses had the same erotic value as with us.

2.- Bas-relief on one of the walls of the Red Chapel, in Karnak temple, with two images of the god Min represented in the usual way: with a feather headdress, his right hand raised and his penis erect. On the left we see how the pharaoh purifies the statue of the god with water, while on the right he does it with incense.

Nor should we forget that the Egyptian people were a very religious people, and the fact that their texts and sacred images have frequent allusions to sex, including incest, adultery, masturbation, homosexuality, and even acts of necrophilia, would have contributed in a decisive way to see sexuality as something completely natural, both in this life and in the other, though still far from this vision of excesses that some later sources wanted to portray.

In the following pages I intend to draw a rough sketch of how this ancient culture approached such an important aspect of human relations, and how that was reflected in their artwork and their writings. And I am aware of the difficulty, if not impossibility, to address the issue moving away from the biases and constraints imposed by the culture in which we now live, very far in all aspects to that which developed along the Nile more than 5000 years ago.

3.- Three musician and dancers depicted in the walls of the tomb of Nakht, "Astronomer o Amun" (XIV c. bC). Tomb TT 52 in the necropolis of the Nobles at Thebes.

4.- Two *ostraca* from the Deir el-Medina where sex scenes have been drawn. The drawings in these supports tend to show much more explicit scenes than those depicted in temples and tombs, which are usually more prudish images. Private Collection and British Museum.

2.- The Study of Sexuality in Ancient Egypt

When studying this important aspect of Egyptian life we must draw on two sources. On one side we find a series of artistic representations in many different formats, and on the other side we have an important number of texts.

When analyzing the texts we have to make a distinction between those that are engraved on the monuments and tombs, which tend to be a little more "prudish," and papyrus writings, which can be of very diverse subjects: from practical books on medicine, teachings, travel stories, dream interpretation, etc., to purely literary works such as stories or poems. Some of these texts can be the most explicit.

With regard to artistic representations, these appear in all sorts of formats. From the reliefs and grand official statuary found in temples, monuments and tombs of royalty and dignitaries, accompanied by paintings with the same aesthetic treatment of eroticism, to the most common items, including amulets, small sculptures and everyday objects that were shaped and decorated with erotic motifs. And, of course, also the drawings on papyrus. We cannot ignore the drawings and engravings found in the stone walls of some quarries and drawn on *ostraca* (small slabs of stone or ceramic on which sketches of drawings or texts were drawn) that often depict the most explicit and carefree sex scenes.

5.- Curious representation that appears in a funerary papyrus of the singer of Amun Henuttawy (c.1070-945 BC), in which we see the god Geb performing autofellatio, and above him we find an arched figure with the body covered with stars in way in which her wife Nut —the sky— is usually represented, but in this case she has been depicted as a man with a huge erect penis, and which is identified with Osiris. British Museum in London.

As in the texts, in images a big difference can be seen between "official" art, in which the only scenes of erotic-sexual nature are usually those featuring the gods, and folk art, in which these scenes are more abundant and often almost reaching the pornographic.

From the available sources there appears to be a chronological difference between written and visual sources because, while most texts with erotic references correspond to the New Empire (XVI-XI century BC), we find the most abundant graphical representations during the Greco-Roman period, beginning in the late fourth century BC, although this should be clarified, as the key work of Egyptian eroticism—the Turin erotic papyrus—is dated between the twelfth and eleventh centuries BC. Although we must not forget that this is a unique document, for the time being.

By studying the documents that have reached us, it is important to consider the audience these were intended for. On the one hand we have the so-called "wisdom literature" or "teachings", documents written by men for men, as it seems established that the vast majority of women were vetoed from learning to read and write. While on the other hand we find the stories and other literary works that were aimed at a wider audience of both genders, which would usually reach them by storytellers and not by direct reading.

In the first are moral and practical advices to men (belonging to the upper class of course) and they are instructed the correct behavior expected of them and the dangers of certain behaviors of women, which are considered unfaithful by nature; whereas the literary texts that we mentioned earlier would be narrated often to a mixed audience, and explain the consequences for the protagonists of behaviors considered incorrect (including those related to the sexual sphere), regardless their sex.

Whatever it may be, the truth is that we generally see a considerable shortage of references and depictions of eroticism and sexuality, especially for older periods. This becomes more evident when we compare the Egyptian culture with others such as Greek, Etruscan and Roman, and that is the reason that after the conquest by Alexander the Great in 332 B.C. erotic depictions in Egyptian art increased in an important way, because the country of the Nile became a part of the Greek world.

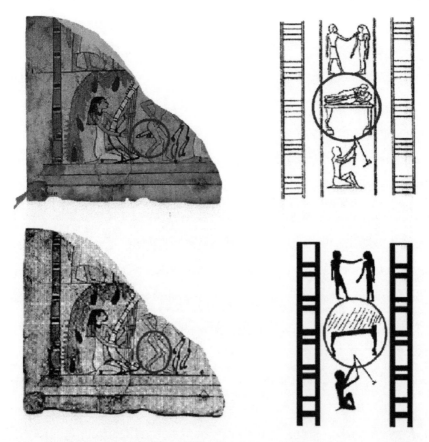

6.- Two examples that perfectly illustrate self-censorship by some researchers when copying or reproducing images with sexual content. To the left, a fragment of painted leather that W.C. Hayes, in a publication in 1990 where he erased the penis hanging from the male figure. On the right, part of a hieroglyphic located in the Beni Hassan II tomb, in Middle Egypt, showing one of the very few images of intercourse with the man lying on top of the woman. P.E. Newberry, when copying it in 1893, removed the couple leaving only the bed.

We must not forget that the first researchers who studied ancient Egypt were not generally as open-minded as ours, so in many cases their attitude towards retrieved pieces with erotic themes vary from indifference or disdain to absolute contempt, which could even lead to their destruction, which has deprived us of many of them. An intermediate position is censorship found in various reproductions of images by the same scholars, of which the parts considered obscene have been eliminated. The striking thing about this is that we find examples of this censorship even in images published in the late twentieth century, something we'd now consider outrageous and totally out of place.

Encoded images.- We indicated that explicit depictions of sex in Egyptian iconography was very low, but in reality it could be much larger than it may seem at first glance, and it's just that many Egyptologists believe that often these intercourses would not be displayed in an open and obvious way, but through the use of symbols and artistic conventions that would be known by their contemporary observers, and that would typically escape us. This would be more frequent in the images depicted in temples and royal tombs, which had to maintain some "decorum," while in the private tombs artists could take some liberties, but not many.

The perfect example is one of the most popular conventionalisms, the godess Isis kite—shaped flying over the mummified body of her husband and brother Osiris or perched on him. Nothing more, but everyone knew that the goddess had had sex with the deceased after transforming into that bird. It suggests what happens but nothing is displayed, it is not necessary, because the story is known to all who see it.

Other conventions considered by investigators as erotic references are not so obvious to us, for example, scenes of fully dressed couples sitting on the bed, which some researchers believe indicate a prelude to the sexual encounter, which of course is not displayed although it is understood. Also fishing scenes in which women appear in the boat dressed in their finery, bejeweled and with wig—something completely illogical in that situation—while the husband throws the harpoon. Some investigators interpret that the launching and nailing of the weapon represents the sexual act.

We should also draw attention to those scenes in which ostentatious women appear wearing wigs, since wigs also seem to indicate the willingness of women for sex. On the papyrus d'Orbiney we find this passage:

"He found me naked all alone. Then he said to me: Come, let us have some time together, let's lie down. Put on your wig".

As we can see we are far from fully understanding the Egyptian mentality and way of dealing with this aspect of life, but we must trust that the advances that are being made, although slower than we would like, will evolve soon into a greater understanding of each and every one of the aspects of this fascinating culture.

7.- Ivory statuette showing a young woman entirely nude. De date it is unknown, maybe from the late Eighteenth Dynasty or early Nineteenth Dynasty (about 1300 BC). Louvre Museum in Paris.

8.- Representation of the god Amun-Min-Kamufet with typical attributes of Min: mummiform aspect, right hand raised, and the erect penis. A peculiarity of this figure in particular is that instead of a feather headdress it presents the white crown of Upper Egypt. Seventh century B.C. Walters Art Museum, Baltimore.

3.- The Gods and Sex

We have already mentioned earlier that one of the reasons why sexuality was seen as a facet of daily life for the Egyptians was the fact that their religion was permeated with sexual episodes. In their cosmogony (part of the mythology which chronicles the birth of the world) and in relations between the gods, sex appeared frequently in all possible expressions, and thus was represented regularly in monuments, tombs and religious papyri with the limitations that we discussed earlier.

The best known of these episodes of sexual tone is also one of the most important because it tells the creation of the world in the Heliopolitan cosmogony (from Heliopolis, *Iunu* for the ancient Egyptians). In it the supreme Egyptian god Atum-Ra, the sun god, created himself out of nothing, and having no woman with which to have offspring masturbated and spilled his semen on the ground. From this semen arose Shu, god of light and air, and Tefnut, goddess of moisture. According to another version the god, when masturbating, received the semen in his mouth, which would represent the feminine part of the act, spitting his two fully formed children. These then sexually joined in a natural way begetting Nut, the sky, and Geb, god of the earth.

Despite being brothers, Nut and Geb had sex continuously, but their father Shu, by order of Ra, forbade this relationship. This is why in artistic representations Nut usually appears arched and covered with stars, on top of Geb who is lying on the ground, and often Shu is between them, separating them. By separating heaven from earth there was space left for the development of life. In some depictions Geb appears with an erection or even performing autofellatio, perhaps as a way to appease his sexual desire toward Nut.

9.- Detail of Butehamon's sarcophagus, preserved in the Egyptian Museum in Turin. We see the goddess Nut, represented as the sky, arched over her husband Geb, the earth, appearing with the erect penis to show his desire towards Nut, which is forcibly separated. Egyptian Museum in Turin.

But the two lovers devised a strategy to unite, if only very occasionally. The ban on them prevented them from being together and having children during the 360 days of the Egyptian calendar, but Nut, with the help of the wise Thoth, got the moon to provide enough light to create five more days (the called epagomenal days). During those five additional days five children were born: Osiris, Horus, Seth, Nephthys, and Isis.

10.- One of the many versions of the scene where the goddess Isis, depicted as a kite, perches on the ithyphallic body of her husband Osiris to have sex with him. After the magical intercourse Osiris will be reborn in the afterlife, while the goddess will become pregnant and will give birth god Horus. Copy of a relief of the temple of Sethi I at Abydos (c. XIII B.C.)

Another myth of major importance in the Egyptian religion is that of Osiris. According to this, Seth killed his brother Osiris, dismembered his body and scattered the pieces throughout Egypt. But Isis, the wife of the deceased, helped by her sister Nephthys and his nephew Anubis, managed to recover almost all the pieces, save for the only part they couldn't recover which was the penis, that had been thrown by Seth to the Nile, where it was eaten by a fish (an Oxyrhynchus). Isis finally managed to recompose the body of her husband creating the first mummy, and replaced the lost member by an artificial one, which allowed her to copulate with him, transformed into a bird, and magically get pregnant. This intercourse also allowed Osiris to rebirth in the afterlife as divinity, while Isis gave birth to Horus, the god represented as falcon-headed, who later became king of Egypt (not to be confused with Horus the Elder, son of Nut and Geb).

As we see, so far all relations are incestuous, and there were no more "human" beings on earth than this group of gods. And it does not end there, because according to Plutarch, Anubis was born of an adulterous relationship between Osiris and Nephthys, wife of Seth. The goddess made Osiris drunk, who as a result slept with her, thinking that he did so with his own wife Isis. With this act Neftis was able to have a son, since Seth, her husband, was infertile.

Another divinity related to sexuality would be Hathor, goddess of women, fertility, love, joy, drunkenness, beauty and sexual enjoyment; let's not forget that for the Egyptian mentality, fertility and pleasure were closely related. In some texts Hathor appears as "Lady of the Vulva" or "Hand of God," the latter epithet associated with Atum's masturbation at the time of creation. Her cult is closely linked with that of Bes, and the Greeks identified her with Aphrodite. Votive offerings were dedicated to her in the form of female figurines with a very marked pubic triangle and wooden phalluses as those found in large numbers in the chapel of Hathor of the Temple of Deir el Bahari.

In erotic poetry they often refer to her as "The Golden One"

"He doesn't know about my desire to embrace him
or he could write to my mother.
Lover, I am bound to you
by *The Golden One* of women.
Come to me so I can see your perfection."
(Papyrus Chester Beatty I, Group A, No. 32)

Min was the god of male sexuality, so was usually depicted as a man with an erect penis. In some sources he is listed as the husband of Hathor, while in others he is considered her son, and at least in the New Kingdom was very present in the coronation rites of the new pharaohs, since to this god was entrusted the potency of the new king and they asked for the birth of the future heir. He was associated with the white bull and with lettuce, which as discussed later was considered a powerful aphrodisiac.

Some authors suggest that originally this god didn't have that consideration of protector of male virility, but would rather be a protective deity trying to stop the dangers with his hand always raised and his permanently erect, threatening penis.

In addition to relations exclusively between the gods, there were also mixed ones between a divine and a human being, who was usually a member of royalty. The best known are those in which a god takes the form of the king to mate with the queen; thus a child was born completely entitled to the throne, since he had been fathered by a god.

The best known examples of such episodes are represented in the temples of Hatshepsut at Deir el Bahari and Amenhotep III in Luxor, and in both cases the queens recognized the god Amun-Ra, who gets in their beds in the form of their husbands, something for which they feel very honored.

On the walls of Deir el Bahari the encounter of the god with the mother of the future Queen Hatshepsut is narrated as below:

"The sublime Amon, lord of the throne of both kingdoms had become her husband, His Majesty, King of Upper and Lower Egypt. He found her asleep in his palace. Awakened by the divine fragrance, she smiled at His Majesty. He then approached her eagerly and was shown in his divine form. She rejoiced at the sight of his beauty. Love flooded her entire body and the palace was filled with the divine sweetness of all perfumes of the Land of Punt"

However, the relationship between the gods and royalty was quite different from those of normal (non-royal or divine) humans, who are instructed to stay away from the sacred buildings for some specific activities. According to Herodotus (II, 64), the Egyptians were the first to ban sex in temples, and not only that, but those who had already done it were forced to wash themselves before entering the sacred precinct again. Meanwhile the priests had to observe several days of sexual abstinence before developing their duties in the temple.

11.- Painted stone statue of Greco-Roman era depicting a man of enormous penis size. This type of figurine became popular in the final stage of the Egyptian world. Private collection.

Phalic cult.- There are many indications of the existence of a phallic cult in ancient Egypt as a symbol of male fertility. Although throughout the history of research in Egypt there have been many attempts to conceal it, if not to destroy it, we still have many pieces of evidence among which are the numerous statues of the gods Bes and Min in ithyphallic position (with an erect penis) that have been found, although the earliest known examples of male figures with a big erect member come from pre-dynastic time.

Herodotus describes in the 5th century B.C. celebrations in honor of Osiris, which he assimilates with Dionysus, and in which the importance of the cult of the phallus in relation to the divinity was evident:

"Egyptians celebrate the rest of the party (in honor of Osiris-Dionysus) with the same apparatus as the Greeks. Instead of phalluses used between the latter, they have invented dolls of a cubit in height, and movable by means of springs, which women take to the streets, obscenely moving and shaking a member almost as big as the rest of the body. (...) The idol's obscene movement and the disproportionate size of that member continue to be a mystery to Egyptians among others of their religion." (History II, 48)

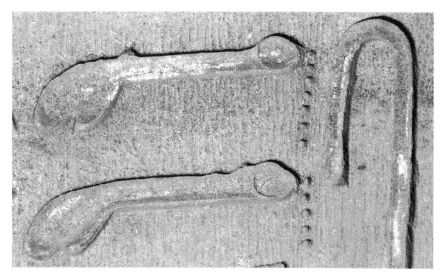

12.- Relief from Kom Ombo temple representing two penises ejaculating. Actually, they are part of a hieroglyphic inscription.

13.- Scene painted on the walls of the tomb of Nebamun (c. XIV B.C.) which depicted the deceased accompanied by his wife and daughter while hunting birds in the swamp. British Museum in London.

4.- Marriage: Of Love and Heartbreak

In ancient Egypt, marriage was considered the ideal status for both men and women, and the nuclear family (the couple with their children) was considered the axis around which Egyptian society should rotate, so even gods were grouped in this way. Such was the importance they gave to this family model that they lacked names to refer to other relatives, for example, the term father was also used to refer to the grandfather, while the same word was used to name the son, grandson and nephew.

In other ancient cultures from the Mediterranean, such as the Greeks or Romans, men tried to prolong their bachelorhood as much as possible, so that for example, for a Greek man, marriage was normal entering the thirties. However, for Egyptian men, that would be too late of an age. In the Teachings of Ani the following is read:

"Take a woman while you are young, for her to make a son to you. She will give birth for you when you are young. Teach your children to be adults. Happy is the man whose people are numerous, he is respected in proportion to his children "(Ani, 6, III, 1-3). Translated by Marc Orriols.

Women would get married younger than men, as they were considered suitable for marriage as soon as they reached puberty, whereas among men it was common to postpone marriage until they achieved a livelihood, and so it was normal for them to marry between 16 and 20 years of age. Studies in contracts from the Ptolemaic period indicate that the most common in that period was for women to be married between 12/13 years of age, although there is clear evidence that this was not always the case and quite younger girls were given in marriage. We have data for the Roman period that speak of girls married at the age of eight, nine and ten, and a mummy (from the late period) had written on its bandages that it corresponded to a married girl of eleven years of age.

This has led many authors to consider that pederasty was common among the ancient Egyptians, something that should be clarified since we can't observe the customs and social standards of a people who disappeared 2,000 years ago through the mentality of a XXI century Westerner. Later we will discuss a quotation from Strabo in which it states as a reason of pride for the parents of a preteen daughter of a good family to exercise sacred prostitution in the temple of Amun.

Let's not forget that, even today, marriages of adults with girls who have not yet reached puberty are quite common in many countries of the world, especially in the Muslim world.

The data we have tells us that among ordinary Egyptians polygamy would be rare, and this happened mainly as a financial issue. As discussed below, in ancient Egypt married women and their children had considerable legal protection, so few men could afford two wives. Yet the wealthy could have more than one, to which some concubines would often be added. Of course, things were very different for royalty, and it was normal for pharaohs to have several wives, often some of them foreign, given in marriage as part of a bond of friendship between states. E.g. written sources tell us that Rameses II had seven wives, including a sister and three of his daughters, and many concubines, which gave him a hundred children throughout his long life (it is estimated that he lived about 92 years). Some researchers have pointed out that by marrying his sister and daughters the pharaoh actually intended to distinguish them with royal dignity rather than being true marriages.

We've also heard about some possible cases of polyandry (a woman with more than one husband), although these are very doubtful. For example, in the tomb of Henet-Nofret the deceased appears accompanied by her two husbands, and in some texts there's also mention of more than one husband. The problem is whether these multiple husbands coexisted in a simultaneous manner or they were successive marriages after the woman became a widow or divorced, something that is not clear, since it is possible for a woman to want to be represented in her grave with her successive husbands in case of a widow. More unusual would be for this to happen in case of divorce.

Because premarital sex seems to have been common and socially accepted without major problems, the virginity of women would not likely be taken into account at the time of marriage. And it was normal for young people (and not so young) to meet in those places known as "beer houses" where attendees danced, sang, played and drank beer, often too much, so it would not be surprising that many couples uninhibited by alcohol ended frolicking into a corner together. Nor would it be unusual to find in these places prostitutes offering their services in a more or less covert way.

Interestingly, despite the great importance that the Egyptians gave to marriage, there's no evidence of wedding ceremonies of any kind. A couple was simply considered married when the spouses began living together, usually after the woman moved to the husband's house. It was actually a simple private agreement that was not registered in any registry, although we believe that, logically an act that was so important for them must have been endorsed in some way, no matter how solemn it was. The one fact, of which there's certainty, is that on the occasion of marriages there were often more or less lavish family parties, with the grandeur of such celebrations depending upon the possibilities presented by the families of the intending spouses.

Another major difference with other contemporary cultures is that, as a general rule, it seems that Egyptian marriages were not imposed by parents, but parental consent itself would be mandatory. In this way, the spouses were often the ones to freely choose the partner with whom they wanted to share their life. Although this doesn't mean that parents didn't influence the choice, especially if we talk about women, considering they could marry when they were still little girls.

We found abundant signs of the affection between young lovers in the many love poems that have come down to us, and that we will explore in more detail later in the chapter dedicated to it.

We also have a considerable number of marriage contracts in which a series of clauses that particularly affect the economics of the new couple are detailed. These contracts did not have to be drawn up at the time of marriage itself, since they could be made later, and began to be written from the eighth century B.C., although they may have already existed before that. They usually included the goods that the new wife would bring home: personal items such as clothing or jewelry, utensils and other household equipment. These objects were owned by the wife, so if they stopped being a couple these would be returned to her, because Egyptians generally separated property, so that each of the spouses still kept their belongings no matter what. In addition, in the case of divorce, the goods acquired during marriage were divided.

In some of the preserved contracts the man pays a sum of money to the family of the bride to formalize the marriage, an amount that could be quite varied. We don't know if this would be done as a sign that his intentions were serious or as "compensation" for the father's losses in work from the daughter.

However in other situations the opposite is the case, and it is the woman who donates an amount to her new husband as payment for her maintenance, and the contract even specifies the amounts he has to spend on her regarding food and clothing, as well as gives guarantees of providing a decent place to live. In case of divorce the husband could choose between returning the money contributed by the woman or continue keeping her even after the split, although this point may be waived in the case divorce occurred as a result of the wife's infidelity.

Curiously "temporary marriage" contracts have also been found, including expiration dates, as shown in this text from Ptolemaic era:

"You will be in my house as long as you're with me as a wife from today, the first day of the third month of the winter season of the year sixteen, until the first day of the fourth month of the flood season of the year seventeen." (Strasbourg's *Ostracon* 1845)

The tradition of temporary marriage still applies today in several countries, including Egypt, but unfortunately this ancient custom has degenerated into a serious problem of covertly child prostitution, in which girls are given in marriage—sometimes just for one day—in exchange for a sum of money that the alleged husband delivers to the "bride's" father as a dowry. Some girls have been through these intended marriages several dozen times.

14.- Explicit graffiti engraved on the wall of a quarry of Wadi Hammamat with a scene of copulation *a tergo*, i.e., with the man penetrating the woman from behind.

In general, the view we get from the preserved marriage contracts is of a relative economic equality between men and women, as both can possess, transmit and manage their properties with great autonomy and without the total submission of women to men that we find in other contemporary and even later cultures. In any case we have to keep in mind that these contracts relate exclusively to partners of a minimally well-off financial situation, so it is unknown how these aspects would treat the lower stratus of society that logically would be the most numerous.

The spouses could dissolve the marriage at the request of

either party, although in some cases this would initiate court proceedings, usually caused by the division of common property, i.e., property acquired during marriage. The causes of divorce could be endless, from infidelity or the sterility of a spouse, to others more curious, as a case in which a man wanted to divorce the woman he had been married for twenty years claiming she was one-eyed, to marry a younger woman who of course has no defect. In the process the wife exclaimed, "After twenty years of living in your house, you suddenly notice that I am one-eyed?"

It was also common for divorced couples to remarry.

But we must not forget that despite the undeniable advantages in marriage for Egyptian women when compared with other Mediterranean cultures, there are also known references of abuse by their husbands and children, and we even have the skeleton of a woman that died at the age of 30-35, buried in the cemetery at Abydos that was used during the Middle Kingdom (2160-1781 BC). She had several fractures in the ribs and left wrist made at different times (but were healed), and she eventually died by a stab wound that entered her back. All this speaks of a history of abuse that only ended with her murder.

It should also be noted a papyrus preserved in the Louvre museum in which it says: "Do not ignore an insult by your wife, hit her. Give her back her property." (Louvre Papyrus 2414, II8-9).

As we see, the man is not only incited to physically abuse his wife in response to insult, but this is also considered grounds for divorce.

To prevent abuse against women by their husbands, some parents did subscribe their future sons in law to oaths in which they pledged not to abuse their wives. For example, we have this document from the time of Ramses III (1184-1153 BC):

"Make Najte-em-Mut to take an oath before the Lord, life, prosperity and health, saying "I will not harm your daughter." Oath before the Lord, life, prosperity and health, that he swears, as Amun endures, as the sovereign endures, if I break my word and harm the daughter of Telmontu at any time, I will receive a hundred blows and be deprived of all profits that I have made with her" (*Bodleian Library Ostracon* 253).

We have even got hold of some documents concerning allegations of ill-treatment, but without information on the penalties on offenders, although everything suggests that these would not be very hard.

Texts have also been discovered that seem to refer to cases of sexual violence against women, out of wedlock of course. Thus, in the Salt papyrus we find the following passage concerning a certain Paneb, of which we will later see charged with multiple cases of adultery:

"(Charge) concerning the fact that stripped Yemenwaw's of her clothes, threw her on top of [a] wall and violated her" (Papyrus Salt 124, r° 1, 19)

Due to the bad state of this part of the papyrus, the reading is not one hundred percent certain and its interpretation is not shared by all researchers.

But in this other text of Diodorus Siculus we did find another clear mention of rape, and its consideration as a particularly serious crime that was punishable as such:

> "The laws regarding women were very severe. The one accused of raping a free woman was to be punished by cutting off the genitals, because it was considered that this crime contained three enormous evil insults in its essence: the insult, corruption of customs, and confusion of offspring" (Diodorus, I, 78).

Although marriages with foreigners were relatively common, in the "wisdom texts" we find frequent warnings about the issues of foreign women. However, it should be understood that a foreigner could also mean a person from another city, and it was considered that when a woman left her natural environment for a strange new place, that she was predisposed to finding a male partner with whom to have sexual intercourse with, regardless of the marital status of either (thus, it was a behavior linked to infidelity).

The only women who appear in these texts as worthy of respect, if not veneration, are mothers. For example in the Teachings of Ani it is said as follows:

> "Fold the meal that your mother gave you, support her as she

supported you. She had a heavy burden with you, but she didn't leave you. When you were born after your months, she was attached to you with her chest in your mouth for three years. While you were growing up and your excrement disgusted her, she didn't get upset saying "What shall I do?" When she sent you to school and you were studying the writings, she kept looking out for you with bread and beer at her home. When you are young take a woman and establish a home, pay attention to your children, take care of them the way your mother had." (*Ani* 38-39, VII, VIII 17, 2). Translation by Marc Orriols.

The most common was for most marriages to occur between people of the same social strata. The union between a free man and a slave was not considered a marriage, she was considered simply a concubine, and even their possible children would be born as slaves. For a man to really want a slave to be considered his wife, he had the option to adopt her, with which she was freed—something he could also do with children born as slaves. Let's not forget that when a woman could not have children it was relatively common to buy a slave with which the husband could have sex with to have a baby which was then adopted by the married couple and raised as their own child.

Sexual relations between the master and the slaves of the house in this sense did not seem to be considered adulterous, but it was rather a prerogative of which he might or might not use.

Adultery.- Extramarital relationships of both partners were frowned upon in Egyptian society, but here the macho mentality was more evident. While an unmarried woman was forbidden to interact with married men and married women were completely denied of extramarital relations, in texts addressing the husband he is only warned against relations with married women but nothing is said of single ones. So, in practice the only one that was completely banned from adultery were women.

With regard to the penalties imposed on adulterers, usually they were harder for women than for men, as it could entail for them even the death penalty, but it seems that in the later period punishments for females were relaxed a lot.

15.- Copy of the figures that appear drawn in a tomb excavated in Deir el-Bahari. By all indications the woman depicted would be none other than the queen Hatshepsut, and the man who penetrates her would be Senenmut, the highest official in the service of the sovereign. There are many indications that in real life both maintained an adulterous relationship.

In any case, penalties for husbands could also prove to be very strict, at least in theory. This can be seen on papyrus 27 from Deir el-Medina, where an individual is warned that if he approach the complainant's woman he was to have his ears and nose cut and be expelled to Kush (Nubia). Yet the individual returned to his old ways and even got his beloved pregnant, so the magistrate now threatens to send him to the quarries of Elephantine if he happens again to have contact with her. There's no mention of the penalties with which he had been threatened on the previous occasion, so it appears they had not been applied.

It is curious that while in some texts, penalties for husbands have appeared, there are no sentences against women, so it is possible that the second case was treated as a family matter in which the husband would be responsible for issuing the penalty on his wife and enforcing it. Something like this seems to be deducted from a story collected in the Westcar papyri dating from the New Kingdom, and in which a priest of whom his wife had been unfaithful appears; the husband had the wife burned (presumably alive) and her ashes thrown into the Nile, while for the man he sought a more imaginative ending: he wanted him to die devoured by a crocodile. The pharaoh approved the measure against the man and it was fulfilled. But let's not forget that this is a story, and we don't know how much is reality versus a type of fable used as a moral lesson.

For the late period, historian Diodorus Siculus did tell us the exact penalties awaiting adulterers, both men and women:

"For the crime of adultery committed without violence, the man was condemned to receiving a thousand blows with a cane, and the woman to have her nose cut: the legislator wanted her to be deprived of her attractiveness as she had only employed it to seduce" (Diodorus, I, 78).

As we see, the historian is clear who is to blame. Still, let's not forget that Diodorus lived in the 1st century B.C., so the customs that he met in Egypt were already strongly influenced by the Greco-Roman world.

But despite the theoretical severity of penalties, adultery was perhaps fairly common, as we have found a large number of court cases and testimonials attesting to this fact, of which a perfect example would be this letter that a worker named Amennakht sent to the vizier accusing Paneb of adultery (the same Paneb whom earlier was accusing abuses to a woman).

"Paneb copulated with citizen Tuy when she was the woman of worker Quenna. He copulated with citizen Huner when she was with Pendua. He copulated with Huner when she was with Hesysunebef; said his son. And when he copulated with Huner, he copulated with Ubkhet, her daughter (hers), and Aapehety, his son, also coupled with Ubkhet". (Papyrus Salt 124, 1° 2'2-4). Translation by Marc Orriols.

As we see, Paneb, besides being an unmitigated adulterer was a big success among women and had a hectic sexual life, of which he even got to involve his son, although we have seen before that his adventures did not end there.

In other "Wisdom texts" authors discouraged revenge for adultery and chose more pragmatic way, as we see in the Teachings of Ankhsesonquis:

"If you find your wife with her lover, get yourself a girlfriend too" (*Ankh.* XIII, 12)

The texts also speak of the consolidated belief among men of the promiscuous nature of women, so they are strongly advised to control their wives so they do not cheat on them with other men, but also suggest men not to approach other men's women to avoid being seduced and induced to adultery.

A final example of the belief Egyptians had about the alleged female fondness towards infidelity is given by Herodotus when talking about a pharaoh who had been blinded:

"(...) For ten years he was therefore blind; but on the eleventh year came an oracle from the city of Buto according to which the time of his punishment had been completed, and he would recover his sight if he washed his eyes with the urine of a woman who had just had sex with her husband and did not know other men. He proved first with his own wife and afterwards when not recovering sight, successively tried with many; and when he finally regained his sight, he gathered the women who had been tested (except the one with which urine he had been washed regaining sight) in a city that is now called Red Earth; and once congregated there, he set fire to the city with all of them inside ..." (Herodotus II, 111)

Incest.- Much has been talked about incest as a common practice among the ancient Egyptians, and that's something we have to clarify.

Although they were not the norm, marriages between siblings existed, and were more frequent in the later periods. Research by Jaroslav Cerny indicate that of 490 marriages studied between the First Intermediate Period (c. 2150-2050 BC) and the Eighteenth Dynasty (c. 1550-1295 BC), he found only two cases of marriages between siblings, something that would change radically later since of 161 marriages from the Ptolemaic period studied, twenty-four percent had been held between siblings, and already in Roman times, during the reign of emperor Commodus (161-192 AD), two thirds of the marriages in the city of Arsinoé were among first-degree relatives (brother-sister and father-daughter).

Incest was also relatively common among royalty, both for political reasons to maintain the royal power within a family, as well as for imitating the gods, among which we have seen that incest was common. But inbreeding could have undesirable results such as congenital malformations and diseases. The best known example is found in the pharaoh Tutankhamun, who carried major health problems during his lifetime, including a foot deformity that caused a pronounced limp, problems quite possibly caused by successive incestuous marriages in his family. The cause of his death appears to have been an infection as a result of a broken leg, which his weak body was unable to fight.

Moreover marriages between non-immediate relatives were quite common in all social classes; mainly they occurred among half-brothers, uncle and nieces, and especially between cousins, which is still prevalent in today's Egypt, and especially in Sudan (ancient Nubia).

A problem faced by scholars is that from the reign of Thutmose III (c. 1490-1436 BC) it began to be common for both boyfriends, girlfriends and husbands to call each other brother and sister, which has generated a lot of confusion.

Harems.- The existence of royal harems is perfectly documented in written sources, iconography and even archaeology, because in Medinet el-Gurob a complete harem was excavated, dating from the New Kingdom. These could be complexes of a huge area, and in them would live together wives and concubines with their children and servants, sometimes in large numbers. To get an idea of the size and capacity that these places could have, we know the example of Princess Tadukhepa of Mitanni, a secondary wife of Amenhotep III (1390-1353 BC), who took with her to Egypt 317 maids, chosen for their beauty. In addition to its residents, a veritable army of guards, scribes and supervisors would work in these areas to ensure proper operation.

It is easy to assume that in their quest to win the favor of the king, underground intrigues and maneuvers would be on the agenda, and the envy and resentment among many women who shared the same goal of bringing heirs to the world would cause many problems. Let's not forget the importance for them to bear children to the monarch, especially those who had chances of reaching the top spot in the line of succession to the crown.

Also harems would often be centers of conspiracies and political maneuvering in order to depose pharaohs or cause changes in dynasty. We know the case of Amenemhat I (1981-1952 BC) who was killed as a result of a conspiracy born in his own harem. Also Ramses III (1186-1155 BC) may have been the victim of a plot to kill him, because a papyrus dated from 1155 B.C., accounts the trial of several members of his harem for plotting to assassinate him. In particular it appears that a secondary wife—Tiyi—tried to kill her husband so that her child Pentaur could ascend to the throne. The conspirators were discovered but the latest studies on the mummy of this pharaoh have detected the presence of a deep cut in the neck that seems to have been the cause of his death, produced that same year, with which it seems evident that conspirators finally managed to successfully complete their purpose, if only in part, because Pentaur never became king.

As noted, harems were heavily guarded and surrounded by high walls to keep strangers out. There is no data to affirm that the guards were eunuchs so it wouldn't be surprising if there was an occasional affair, and this would have to go back to what was said earlier on the importance of having children. It is easy to assume that more than a few pretended sons of pharaohs arose from such affairs, but those children, legitimate or not, could secure the future of their mothers if they were assumed to be of royal blood.

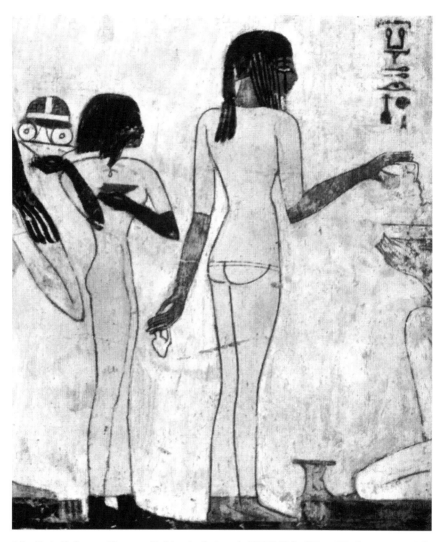

16.- Detail decoration on Rekhmira's tomb (TT100) in West Thebes. Two girls serve food and drink at a banquet (XVIII dynasty).

17.- Copy of a scene from the tomb of Puyenré in Thebes, which depicted the deceased copulating with his wife. His sexual organs are shown as an exact copy of the hieroglyph meaning to copulate, shown on the right.

5.- Gynecology, Aphrodisiacs, Contraception and Abortion

For the Egyptians, as for most of the peoples of antiquity, children were of vital importance, so tremendous value was given to fertility. The ideal woman was one that could easily conceive and successfully complete pregnancy and feeding her children, while in men sexual potency, coupled with the ability to procreate, were major factors.

This importance was closely related to the high rate of infant mortality that occurred in antiquity, where it was common for half of born children not to live past the first years of life. The more children were born the more they would survive to work the fields, take care of the parents when they were elderly, provide them a decent burial and continue the funeral rites after their death.

That's why medical and magical Egyptian texts are full of allusions, remedies and spells designed to favor births and combat infertility. Unlike other cultures in Egypt there is no known reference of the practice of infanticide.

Knowledge of medicine in general, and more specifically on gynecology and urology, were advanced for their time among the Egyptians, though not so much as popular belief attached to them. We know that the penis was known as *henen*, and was always represented erect, while the vagina is called *Kat* (mortar), and was depicted in hieroglyphics as such. The uterus was called *sed*; and for the embryo in general, whether human or animal, the word *suhet* (ovule) was used, while *wenu* was a exclusive name for the human embryo.

They knew the role of semen in the fertilization of women but did not know its exact origin because they thought it came from the spinal cord, from where it would reach the testicles through ducts. They knew that for fertilization to occur it was necessary for a man's semen to penetrate inside the woman, although it wasn't very clear for them that it had to reach the ovaries. According to Egyptologist Lise Manniche, it seems they thought it just had to go inside the female body by any of the natural orifices, either the vagina, anus, mouth or even the ear.

They also believed that many female ailments such as muscle aches and pains in the teeth and mouth originated in the vagina, which on the papyrus Kahun the following can be read:

"For a woman whose eyes are aching till she cannot see, on top of aches in her neck:
You should say of it 'it is discharges of the womb in her eyes'.

You should treat it by fumigating her with incense and fresh oil,

fumigating her womb with it, and fumigating her eyes with goose leg fat.

You should have her eat a fresh ass liver."

From this highly questionable knowledge, ancient Egyptians devised a series of contraceptive methods of very different real utility.

Contraceptives.- The simplest birth control system has always been the "*coitus interruptus*" i.e. ejaculation outside the body of the woman. Despite the lack of explicit allusions we believe it was quite possibly one of the preferred methods in Egypt despite risk of failure. And in Egypt "*coitus interruptus*" lacked the negative connotations that existed in other cultures such as Jewish, in which it was even expressly prohibited by law (remember the passage of Onan in the Old Testament). In the land of the Nile it was not only not prohibited, but as we have seen before the fact that spilling semen was at the origin of the creation of the world according to Heliopolitan cosmogony. For the same reason male masturbation would not be frowned upon.

Another simple method recommended in some papyri, and also of limited usefulness, would be douching after intercourse.

To prevent sperm to penetrate into the body of the woman they devised various blocking systems that could be considered precarious precursors of today's diaphragms. The simplest was to simply introduce a ball of cotton or linen in the bottom of the vagina, for which long forceps that have been located sometimes as part of toiletries material of Egyptian women would be used. There are even papyri in which servants specialized in removing these balls using tweezers are mentioned. Some texts indicate that the extracted cottons were then burned in the yard of the houses.

An improved version of the previous system was the use of certain products with alleged spermicidal properties, with which these pieces of cotton or linen were soaked. Among the formulas used the famous medical papyrus Ebers mentions a mix of acacia yolks with honey, which once introduced into the vagina could provide contraceptive effects even for several years. Modern analysis have been found that the acacia contains a type of latex that during fermentation produces lactic acid, a substance that is among the components of some of spermicides used today. Another formula consisted of a mixture of honey with Natron.

It is also advised in some of these texts the use of *auti*, a powder obtained from the stems of a tree similar to the rubber tree which was used in a somewhat strange formula, as it was mixed with crocodile dung and shaped cylindrically to be inserted into the vagina before intercourse.

Obviously today no sane gynecologist would ever prescribe this method of contraception to patients, although some researchers argue that this preparation has some scientific basis, since feces modify the acidity of the vaginal mucosa, which could kill sperm.

Another method mentioned in the surviving texts is to

smoke the vagina and uterus with medicinal plants. For that, women sat over a brazier in which herbs were laid. Other papyri indicate to use bellows which were breathed "until the smoke came out of the mouth of the woman." No comment.

The Berlin Medical Papyrus recommends some contraception methods using smoke but also include an oral intake. When a woman wants to avoid pregnancy:

"You have to smoke out her vagina with grass seed to prevent her from receiving the semen. Then you will create a prescription for her to release the semen: 5 parts oil, 5 parts celery, 5 parts sweet beer, warm it up and drink for four mornings. " (Meskell, 2005: 141).

In some texts it is indicated that babies should be breastfed until they are three years old. Since (at least in theory) while the woman is breastfeeding ovulation doesn't occur, and therefore pregnancy cannot occur, this long-term breastfeeding may also have been used as a precarious contraceptive method, although it should be kept in mind that from the sixth month the effectiveness of this system decreases progressively.

Other methods that are mentioned in the texts still have less utility and some are quaint if not extravagant: vigorously jumping or squatting right after intercourse to expel semen, hold the breath while ejaculation occurs, sneezing or drinking something cold.

Although it is easy to find on the Internet reports that suggest that the ancient Egyptians invented condoms and that several types of these have been found in excavated graves, the fact is that there is no evidence that this is so, and the closest thing we have identified are penis guards made of fabric that would not be useful as a means of contraception.

Abortion.- In ancient medical texts there are frequent quotes indicating the importance of carrying the pregnancy to good term and to avoid premature birth, as well as the dangers these involved, for which people didn't hesitate to use spells and other magical practices since they considered that the god Seth was responsible for failed pregnancies. With these practices they treated to avoid at all cost the "flooding," as abortion is called on a papyrus preserved in London because of the large blood spill that often accompanies fetal loss.

Recipes have also been found to prevent childbirth loss, which were made of plants mixed with honey and oils or onions with wine, and that were applied inside the vagina in case of bleeding. With them it was intended to shrink the womb to retain the fetus in the mother's body.

But on the other hand we also find references to induced abortion, which is referred to as "deviation of pregnancy," so everything suggests that, although frowned upon, it would be a fairly common and socially tolerated practice. To achieve this objective, the Ebers Papyrus recommended crushing acanthus fruits, dates and onions, mix that paste with honey and spread it on a cloth to be applied in the vulva of the woman. Another method used would be douching with various preparations, among which hot oil is highlighted.

Since in Egypt children were considered a blessing, it is estimated that abortion would be a fairly rare practice, perhaps restricted mostly to women with medical problems and other females who for certain reasons wouldn't or couldn't become pregnant, such as perhaps prostitutes.

We also know various methods to promote fertility and some "tests"—both for pregnancy as well as for fertility—that are quite curious.

Fertility and pregnancy tests.- The Egyptians believed that the mouth, vagina and anus openings were conduits that converged into the belly, where they intercommunicated. So they devised a simple way to tell if a woman was or not fertile; a clove of garlic or onion was introduced into the vagina of a woman—and the next morning her mouth would be smelled. If the breath smelled of garlic or onion it meant that this woman could become pregnant, otherwise it was considered that her internal tubes were clogged, so that the woman could not conceive.

Another fertility test is to orally administer to the patient date flour mixed with beer or a mixture of herbs with milk from a woman who had given birth to a son; if the woman vomited the preparations she was considered not sterile. As a curiosity, it may be noted that they also thought that cross-eyed women were unable to conceive a child, although we ignore the reasons for such an idea.

It was considered that the milk of a woman who just gave birth to a boy was excellent to promote female fertility, but also to heal burns, eye problems and treat childhood diseases such as diarrhea, pneumonia, bronchitis, etc.

With regard to pregnancy tests, according to the Kahum papyrus the most common was to wrap in a cloth a few grains of wheat and barley which were then soaked with urine of a woman. If both seeds germinated the woman was pregnant, if none germinated then the woman was not pregnant and if only one germinated then the test had to be redone.

18.- Main protective gods of pregnancy and childbirth. From left to right: Hathor, Bes and Taweret. Diverse origins.

This test also offered the possibility of knowing whether the future child would be a boy (if the wheat germinated first) or a girl (if barley germinated first).

Researchers believe that the first part of the test has some scientific basis, since the hormones in the urine of a pregnant woman can stimulate seed germination, however the part that tries to predict the gender of the offspring lacks the slightest scientific basis or reliability.

Childbirth.- In such a religious and superstitious society as the Egyptian, a time and an event as dangerous as pregnancy and childbirth could not be developed turning their backs to the gods, to which the woman was entrusted so that everything went as well as possible. Although the mother goddess was naturally Hathor, ordinary people believed she was a busy goddess, so often they sought the help of other lesser gods, mainly Taweret and Bes, who were considered guardians of the home, pregnancy and childbirth. Taweret was a goddess who was depicted as a hybrid creature with lion's paws, crocodile back and female hippopotamus body, usually pregnant. She could have the head of a hippopotamus or a woman. Meanwhile Bes was a grotesque dwarf with fat body, big ears and puffy cheeks, but with a gentle and friendly appearance.

Of course there would be no shortage of amulets, many with the image of these gods and their attributes.

Also have been found recipes for preparations that would supposedly work to induce labor, such as saffron powder mixed with beer, a mix which had to rubbed on the belly of the pregnant woman. Applying a compresses of hay and reeds was also recommended.

The normal way in which women gave birth was to

position themselves kneeling or squatting on the floor or on some bricks with a ritual function. These magical bricks were similar to those that were placed in some tombs, with which, using clear symbolism, the rebirth of the deceased in the afterlife was sought. In some reliefs the mother is portrayed being helped by several goddesses, but in real life they would be aided by midwives and often by other female relatives or neighbors, even if they were not specialized in this work. (The hieroglyph representing the idea of giving birth is a woman kneeling, with the head and arms of a newborn poke out).

19.- Small bas-relief on stone with hieroglyphic that represents the idea of giving birth. A woman kneeling with child poking his head and arms under her. The two elements that are under the mother are sacred bricks, on which was common to stand during childbirth. British Museum.

To mitigate the pain of childbirth medical papyri recommend giving the mother liquor and beer to get her drunk.

Deliveries would take place within the home or in a building erected specifically for that function. These were simple pavilions with four wooden poles and a light covering that would be erected in the garden of large estates or on the roof of the simplest houses.

The Westcar papyrus refers to a period of purification of two weeks after delivery, which would help women to rest and avoid infections caused by injury from childbirth. This practice was common in other ancient cultures, as well.

It seems that outside the town of Deir el-Medina there was a "women's place," a construction where women in labor and their babies would retreat during these two weeks. Interestingly women who were menstruating would also be found in there, equally considered impure, so we assume that it would be quite a busy, lively place.

In a medical papyrus it is recommended to apply new oil into the vagina to facilitate healing of damage from delivery.

Other medical remedies.- We have already commented that extending breastfeeding up to three years was recommend and we also find references to preparations and methods to promote the production of breast milk. One of the most curious is to rub the back of the new mother with oil in which a Nile perch had been fried.

It was also considered that the mice had healing properties and it was recommended for the mother to eat fried mouse, as the healing power of the same would pass to the baby through breast milk. And mice seemed to be almost a panacea, as they were also prescribed to cure coughs or prevent graying.

Unlike other remedies that appear in the text, the use of mice for medicinal purposes has been proven by archaeology, as in the stomachs of several deceased children in pre-dynastic time in Upper Egypt, the anthropologist G. Elliot Smith found traces of these rodents, with which children had been fed in a last attempt to save their lives.

Also menstrual blood was considered a healing element of the first order, and women who wanted to counteract the effects of gravity—and aging—were recommended to rub their breasts with this menstrual blood to keep them upright. Similarly it is recommending to rub infants with this blood to ward off evil spirits.

Another practice that seems to have been common to know the chances of survival of a sick child was to give the child a piece of crushed placenta mixed with milk. If he ate it without problems it was a sign that the child would live, but if he didn't swallow, or vomited it, it meant he would die.

This was not the only way used to know the fate of babies. The famous Ebers Papyrus indicates that if the first sound produced by a newborn when crying was "*ni*" he would live, but if it was "*ba*" then he would die without remedy. It says nothing of other possible syllables.

The deaths of women during pregnancy and childbirth were frequent, which caused their life expectancies to be lower than that of men. We have data from the necropolis of Saqqara indicating that while men buried there had died at an average age of 33 years, women had been buried at the age of 29 on average. This age difference is maintained at inquiries carried out in other places, for example, from the study of 290 labels on mummies from Roman times preserved in the Louvre, in which the age of the deceased was written, it shows that the average age at death for men was 27, while that of women was 22. Yet this difference in life expectancy by gender was less than in other ancient cultures, for example between the Iberians the difference was around 10 years, which is about twice.

Menstruation.- We have already commented that women were considered impure while they were menstruating, so at that time they would abstain from sex. From Deir el-Medina more information has survived about how Egyptian women dealt with their periods. For example, listings of the clothes carried to laundries have been found in which the so called "behind bands" are listed, which were a kind of compress made with linen. Of course, they would be reused after washing.

We also know of the absence of women from their homes during these days (remember that they remained in the "women's place") could eventually cause disorders on the husbands' work.

This is indicated in records from the same town of Deir el-Medina where workers attendance to their jobs in the Valley of the Kings was monitored. Records have been found indicating that some individuals had missed work for several days because they had to attend their home because their wives were on their period in the "women's place".

Aphrodisiacs and love potions.- The Egyptians believed that certain foods and substances have aphrodisiac properties, and thus appear in medical treaties and other texts.

It seems that the best known aphrodisiac was lettuce, especially serriola variety whose trunk secretes a sperm-like fluid. Scientific studies have confirmed that moderate amounts of lettuce stimulate sexual appetite while curiously inhibit it in large quantities because it has soothing and sedative effects. Let's remember that this plant was associated with the god Min, who was represented with a permanent erection.

Other foods that were considered to stimulate sexual desire would be pomegranate, ginger, fennel, coriander marinated in wine or radish mixed with honey. Actually honey should be considered a stimulant itself, as it has been shown that it maintains high levels of testosterone while decreasing estrogen.

We can't forget the blue lotus of the Nile, which in addition to functioning as a sexual stimulant has narcotic properties that would certainly be exploited; it was also a symbol of sex of the highest order, as we can see in the Turin papyrus, in which it adorns the heads of most of the women who appear in its sex scenes. Chemical analysis performed in the Museum of Manchester have shown that in this flower can be found substances that act the same way as the active ingredient of Viagra. Could the blue color of the famous pill come from it?

The mandrake is also on the list of plants with hallucinogenic and aphrodisiac powers.

In the papyri we also find remedies for male impotence. For example there is a prescription in the Ebers papyrus entitled "weakness of the male organ," for which a preparation is recommended that includes a large number of ingredients, including henbane, weeping willow, juniper, acacia, myrrh, goose fat, watermelon, pig feces, etc. With this mix a poultice was prepared that should be applied around the penis.

For women to enjoy sex more, in a papyrus (British J. M. 10070 and Leiden 383) it is recommended to rub the penis of the man with the foam from the mouth of a stallion just before bedtime. This same papyrus also contains other preparations to acquire the love of a woman, to force a woman to enjoy sex, and to separate a man from a wife or a woman from her husband.

Lastly, we found some extravagances allegedly designed to increase sexual desire, like drinking dissolved pearls in wine or applying ointments made from baboon excrement... Although I doubt that most people feel the slightest sexual stimulation to see their partner cover in monkey feces.

In addition to these preparations we would have to take

magic into account, which was of enormous importance in all aspects of life of the ancient Egyptians, so it was common to use spells and charms to improve sexual performance and attract the attention of the beloved.

In some cases these spells were used in a conjunction with medical treatments to strengthen them, as in this case of a spell intended to increase a patient's potency. Despite being information from a very fragmented papyrus, we can read that while the member was smeared with a preparatory substance, the following incantation had to be recited:

"Greetings, great God, who created the upper class. You, Khnum, you set the lower class. You can try (...), the mouth of each vulva, be erect, do not be limp, be strong, do not be weak ... You (...), strengthen the testicles with Seth, son of Nut". (Papyrus Chester Beatty X)

From Ptolemaic times have come down to us a number of sheets of lead with spells and curses of all kinds. What interests us are those texts in which it is intended that a person, whether male or female, would fall surrendered to the charms of the one whom makes the spell. Often the request includes taking potential competitors out of the way.

"I bind you, Teodotis, daughter of Eus, at the tail of the snake and crocodile's mouth and the ram's horns, and the venom of the cobra and cat hair, and to the God's penis, so that you can never have sex with another man nor have sexual contact, or

vaginal or anal, nor give a fellatio, nor obtain pleasure with another man, but instead only with me, Amonion son of Hermitaris. Carry out this enchantment of binding of Teodotis, the same used by Isis, so that Teodotis, daughter of Eus will never experience another man, but just me, Amonion. Let her come flying, submissive, mad with passion, looking for Amonion son of Hermitaris, and to bring her thigh to my thigh, her genitals to mine in eternal exchange, during the time of her life." (SGD 161. Egypt, exact provenance unknown)

20.- Terracotta female figurine from Ptolemaic era, to which thirteen bronze needles were nailed. It was found inside a jar beside a lead sheet with a curse against a woman. Louvre Museum.

The sheets with engraved spells, common in the Greek world, were often buried in the cemeteries, because normally the intercession of certain deceased or the gods of the afterlife was requested; at other times they were thrown into pits or caves as they felt that these holes communicated with the underworld. Sometimes these spells were accompanied by lead, wax or terracotta figurines with needles stuck in various parts of the body, just as we see in voodoo practices.

Egyptians also took the calendar into account, as they felt there were days that were more or less conducive to the performance of any activity, and sex of course would be included. For example, according to the Westcar papyrus, the fifth day of the month of Paofi was not conducive to love and sex and includes this curious warning:

> *"Don't leave home for any side, and do not have relations with women (...) The child born on this day would die of excessive sexual pleasures."*

Circumcision, sexually transmitted diseases and other ailments.- The studied medical texts show that sexually transmitted diseases don't appear to have been a major problem in ancient Egypt, and only gonorrhea has been documented with some assurance, for which the Ebers Papyrus advises to use *Cannabis Sativa*, which is to be crushed, mixed with honey and applied inside the vagina. The antibiotic effect of the *cannabis'*

alkaloids is scientifically proven, and in 1907 the recognized treaty of pharmacopoeia "*Merck Index*," recommended an emulsion of *cannabis* seeds to treat some of the effects of gonorrhea.

The same Ebers Papyrus recommends for "sick breasts" (it doesn't specify what particular disease) to be treated with a mixture of cow brains, wasp droppings and calamine, with which a plaster was prepared. The breasts would be covered with it for four days.

The medical papyri also describes cancer of the cervix, adding that it was detected by the smell coming from the vagina.

To treat vaginal infections medical papyri prescribe diverse mixtures with which the diseased area should be irrigated, and among its ingredients we find donkey milk, pig's bile or crushed cow horn.

According to the Ebers Papyrus a displaced uterus could be repositioned by burning dried human excrement in a censer while the woman stood over it with her legs open so the smoke could penetrate through her vagina. The Egyptians had the idea that this organ floated freely in the womb of the woman, and if it positioned itself in the wrong place, could cause various ailments.

Circumcision was a common practice among Egyptian men, and it was so from predynastic time, as naturally mummified bodies dating from the Naqada I period (c. 3900 BC) have been found to be circumcised, although we should consider it to be more of a religious rite than a medical intervention, so it was carried out by priests and not by doctors. This operation was carried out always with a curved flint knife despite having available much more sharp metal instruments. Circumcision would be seen as a rite of passage for children to adulthood.

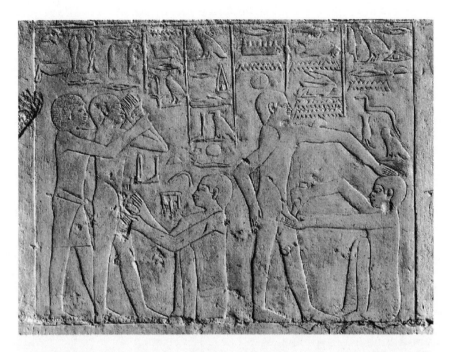

21.- Relief from the tomb of Ankhmahor, in Saqqara, with circumcision scene. While an individual is bandaging the penis of one of the young men another seems to make a cut on the penis of the second one.

In a well known relief from the tomb of Ankhmahor (VI Dynasty, 2345-2181 BC) it is clearly recorded the circumcision of two teenagers; an individual grabs from behind one of the young men while another, kneeling before him, seems to be bandaging the penis; next to it a second young man stands before another man who grabs his penis with his left hand while with the right hand seems to be making a cut with a knife. In a relief from the Khonspekhrod Temple in Karnak, a similar scene appears, but is not as well preserved, and is missing the top half of the figures.

Some Egyptologists such as Marc Orriols believe that the circumcision that was practiced in ancient Egypt was not the typical circular one of the Jewish world, in which a section of the foreskin is cut so that the glans is completely uncovered, but another mode in which a cut was made on the top of the foreskin so that it opens and is collected under the glans. Some images seem to agree with the Spanish author, including the aforementioned tomb of Ankhmahor, where apparently a priest is practicing a cut lengthwise on top of the boy's penis. This type of circumcision is still practiced today in parts of Africa, as among the Masai.

Although common, circumcision doesn't seem to have been a mandatory practice, since the historian Herodotus indicates that priests had to be circumcised, which shows that there were men who were not.

Also when studying the mummy of Pharaoh Ahmose (XVIII Dynasty, 1549-1524 BC) it was found that he had not been circumcised, and it is not an isolated case.

There are some references to "uncircumcised virgins," while the Greek geographer Strabo states:

"One of the most zealous customs observed among Egyptians is this, they raise each child that is born (i.e., they don't practice infanticide), circumcise boys and practice excision on girls". (Book XVII, 2,5)

This suggests the existence of female circumcision,

although we have no specific data that allows us to know what this operation exactly consisted of, as in places where it is practiced it can range from a simple symbolic puncture on the clitoris to complete removal of this organ along with labia minora and majora. Studies performed so far on mummies of women have not found any evidence of manipulation in their genitals, although it should be noted that these operations are difficult to detect in the mummified bodies.

22.- Relief from the inner northern wall of the Temple of Khonspekhrod at the Precinct of Mut, (Luxor), representing a scene of circumcision (XVIII dynasty).

23.- Ptolemaic era figures made on different supports representing sexual and phallic scenes. Various sources.

6.- The Sexual Practice: What did Egyptians Like in Bed

As we see, it appears that Egyptians enjoyed sex without complexes or guilt. Fertility was very important and this was inseparable from sexual pleasure, which is why they would take care of their looks to be more attractive to the opposite sex. For instance, it is known that Egyptians of both sexes were accustomed to shave the whole body, with body hair being considered a symptom of unattractiveness in grooming and personal hygiene.

Sex positions.- We said earlier that there are very few graphic depictions of sex among the ancient Egyptians except for the already mentioned Turin papyrus, and interestingly a significant number of them show copulation *a tergo*, i.e., with the man penetrating a woman from behind, often with both partners standing. This has led some researchers to argue that this would be the "canonical" position in Pharaonic Egypt, which seems to be corroborated by some texts.

24.- Drawings on *ostraca* in which sexual scenes are represented where the man enters the woman from behind, what is known as copulation *a tergo*, from Deir el-Medina; and part of a hieroglyph representing the "missionary" position, from the tomb of Beni Hassan II. Copy by K. Lepsius.

The hardest thing is to distinguish whether these drawings represent scenes of vaginal or anal sex, which has given rise to various theories and interpretations since, for example, between 190 cultures around the world studied at the time by Frank A. Beach and Clellan S. Ford (Patterns of Sexual Behavior, 1955), they found no culture in which copulation *a tergo* was predominant. That has led more than one researcher to think that what is depicted in these images are scenes of anal sex, and the artists were trying to emphasize that they were sexual relations for pleasure, to distinguish them from those held in order to reproduce which would be represented in other positions.

This is not supported by other authors who, while not denying that some of these images actually show anal copulation, consider these mostly refer to vaginal sex. And as evidence they show some quotes and ancient texts in which it is stated that this was the "Egyptian style" when it comes to sex. Another example is found in the Dester Beatty papyrus, which tells how the goddess Anat could not prevent Seth from "riding on his behind covering her as does a ram" (VII, 5-11, 3). But we must bear in mind that Seth is frequently associated with behaviors of brute force, almost animal-like, as befits the god of chaos, the desert and injustice.

Another position which would be very common is the one known by us as "missionary," i.e., the woman lying face up and the man above. We find it in very few graphic representations, such as the tomb of Khety in Beni Hassan where, also, it's not a scene itself but part of a hieroglyph. Apart from these few drawings, this position is mentioned in some texts, but always indirectly, and they implied that it would be a common position. For example, in a papyrus preserved in the Louvre, Isis narrates the intercourse with Osiris as follows:

"I'm your sister Isis. There is no god or goddess who has done what I've done. I have taken the place of a man, although I am a woman, so your name will live on earth, since your divine sperm was in my body."

Isis indicates that she has taken the place of man, since she was forced to copulate with his late brother positioning herself above him, if only in the form of a bird. It clearly implies that the normal thing was for the man to position himself on top of the woman.

In Coffin Texts we find another reference which shows that the man lies on top of a woman:

"He will copulate in this land day and night; then the woman's orgasm will arrive under him whenever he copulates"(CT 576, VI 191, l-n).

In the iconography only two scenes are known, though often repeated, in which a woman is shown copulating by lying on top of a man, and both deal with the deities Isis and Nut. In both cases the woman is placed on top of a man because it is the only possible position; in the first one because Osiris is dead; in the second one the exception is motivated by the conception of the cosmos, in which the goddess Nut represents the celestial dome, which is located at the top, while her partner, Geb, the Earth, is at the bottom.

Masturbation.- We discussed at the beginning of this work that male masturbation in Egyptian culture doesn't have the negative connotations found in others since, according to the Heliopolitan cosmogony, it was used by Re-Atum for nothing less than to create the world, so that representations of this god ejaculating and his children Shu and Tefnut rising from the spilled semen are not rare.

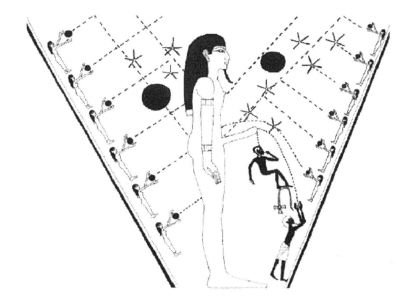

25.- Representation of Atum at the time of the creation of humanity according to the Heliopolitan cosmogony. The god masturbates, and from his semen Shu and Tefnut, the first divine couple, emerge. The twelve small goddesses represent the twelve day and night hours. Copy from the tomb of Ramses VI (XX Dynasty) in the Valley of the Kings at Thebes.

It seems that this creative act was reproduced by some kings in an annual ceremony in which the king would masturbate until ejaculating on the Nile, which acquired a fertility in this way that was then transferred to Egypt. According to other sources, the

Queen would be the one in charge of relieving the Pharaoh in this ritual, and we must not forget that one of the religious titles held by many Egyptian queens and princesses was "Hand of the God," which made them responsible for rites related to sexual stimulation of Amon, in which they represent the feminine aspect of creation, that is, the hand with which the god masturbated.

While there are very few references to male masturbation, the ones regarding female masturbation are simply nonexistent. And although there are many objects found with phallic appearance and which may well have been used by Egyptian women to get some fun moments, most were no more than simple amulets propitiatory to fertility. Of course, one use doesn't have to necessarily exclude the other.

It is easy to find online stories like the alleged precursor of the vibrator used by Queen Cleopatra, for which several bees were introduced into a metal box. It is assumed that the vibration produced by the buzz was transmitted to the walls of the box, which applied at the right point would give the Queen solitary pleasure. This story lacks the slightest historical basis.

Oral sex.- Allusions and representations of this sexual practice are mostly scarce, limited almost entirely to some paintings in which the god Geb appears doing autofellatio upon the impossibility to maintain sex relations with his wife Nut. The fact that the god relieved himself in this acrobatic and impractical way rather than by a simple masturbation, seems to indicate that oral sex was a common practice among the Egyptians, although it wouldn't appear in artistic representations, for being a sterile practice that didn't pursue reproduction. This is also another example of how one thing was the official position (no pun intended), while the sexual lives of most Egyptians was quite different.

26.- Curious scene on the papyrus of Ani representing a woman weeping at a mummy. At first glance it may seem that the woman is actually giving a fellatio to the deceased, which is physically impossible, because if we take a closer look, the right arm and legs of the woman are behind the mummy, meaning she is not in front of the mummy but in a more distant plane. What seems like the penis inside the mouth of the woman is actually her left arm stretched to, in an impossible position, hug the waist of the mummy. For the author, there is no doubt that the artist sought to show the optical effect of a fellatio without actually painting it. British museum.

We also find a curious representation on a papyrus of the Book of the Dead of Ani, preserved in the British Museum in London, where a woman is kneeling with her mouth slightly open up to the genitals of a mummified man. For some it is simply a plaintive mourning the death of the represented man, although with characters painted oddly close to each other, while for others this would be clearly fellatio, of course, performed *postmortem*. If we look closely at this picture we can see that what looks like the mummy's penis in the mouth of the woman, is actually part of her arm, though painted in a way that looks like oral sex. Our view is that the painter deliberately sought the illusion to show fellatio without actually painting it.

We will discuss under the section dedicated to necrophilia how sexual intercourse with corpses was not something totally strange between the Egyptians and in some cases had clear religious implications.

Zoophilia.- In written sources, especially those from a later period, various allusions to this sexual practice appear. And here again we see how their origin lies in mythology, where we find several episodes in which the gods have relations with animals or other gods taking the form of an animal. Among the many examples found we can again cite the goddess Isis. According to some accounts, after recomposing the body of Osiris by joining its pieces and mummifying it, she took the form of a kite to copulate with him magically.

In other sources a wide variety of animals are collected with which both men and women would have sex, and among them the bull should be noted, with which women would copulate, and the crocodile, which appears as a sexual partner both for men and women. This caught the attention of the Greek and Roman historians. Lets see how the Greek historian Herodotus tells of one of these sexual encounters with a ram, which he witnessed during his visit to the country of the Nile in the 5th century BC:

"In that nome (Mendes) a monstrosity occurred in my days, a he-goat had intercourse openly with a woman. This was publicly known and applauded". (Book II, 46)

This event that shocked the Greek scholar had occurred during the annual festival dedicated to the god Knum, and as he says, it didn't surprise anyone as it was common during that celebration.

Necrophilia.- This practice, which today we consider a deviant behaviour, seems to have been something not strange in ancient Egypt, although even then it would be neither legally nor socially acceptable.

Classical sources indicate that when wealthy families gave a deceased woman to the embalmers, they entrusted a person with the responsibility for supervising the corpse to prevent it from being profaned, and Herodotus tells us that the Egyptians used to not deliver the corpses of beautiful women to embalmers until after three or four days, when the putrefaction of the corpse had began. Logically, this would cause the embalming process to not obtain optimum results, which could be the cause of the poorer conservation observed in some female mummies compared to male ones.

Presumably, these measures would also be adjusted to the conditions of the deceased. It would not be necessary to take the same precautions with a seventy year old woman compared with a teenage girl in the prime of life.

The origin of these necrophilic practices in Egypt—putting deviations aside—is found again in their mythology. Noting the episode discussed in the previous section, in which Isis copulates with Osiris after he had died, and the goddess gave him an artificial penis that replaced the one that Seth had thrown into the Nile.

27.- Detail decoration on Djoserkareseneb's tomb in West Thebes. Two very Young nude girls attend the guests in a banquet

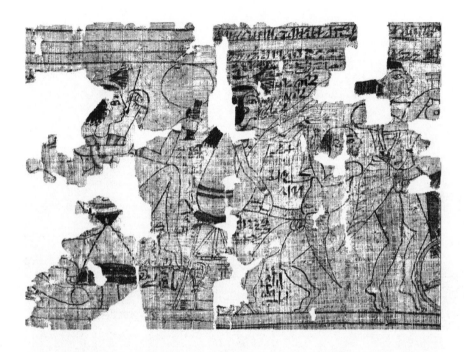

28.- Fragment of the Turin Erotic Papyrus in which some of its scenes can be partially appreciated. Unfortunately deterioration, after almost two centuries of bad storage and handling, is evident. Egyptian Museum in Turin.

7.- The Erotic Papyrus of Turin

It is without doubt the most explicit and recognized representation of sex scenes from ancient Egypt, but despite its importance it has remained hidden almost to this day in the stores of the Egyptian Museum of Turin, since it was not until 1973 that it was published in full by J. Omlin, yet it took many years before it was finally exposed in their showcases.

Papyrus 55001, as it is officially known, was part of an important collection of Egyptian antiquities that in 1824 was sold by the adventurer, antiques dealer and French consul Bernardino Drovetti (Piedmont 1776 Turin 1852) to then King Charles of Savoy. Drovetti would obtain the items both in his own excavations and through acquisition with the many professional tomb looters that swarmed Egypt back then. The exact origin of the papyrus is unknown, although it appears that originally it would have been placed in a tomb of the necropolis of Deir el-Medina, the town where the artisans and artists who built and decorated the tombs of the nearby Valley of the Kings at Thebes lived. Has been dated between 1186 and 1070 BC

As we see elsewhere in this book, from Deir el-Medina also came various sexual scenes drawn on *ostraca*, so it appears that there was a major workshop for production of material with erotic content, if not pornographic, that would be provided to wealthy Egyptians of that time, ones who could afford to buy objects of the same quality as the papyrus we have at hand, since the drawings are made with remarkable skill, much higher than other scenes of a sexual nature that appear in *ostraca and graffiti*.

That same year of 1824 the papyrus was examined by the famous French Egyptologist Jean-François Champollion, the decipherer of hieroglyphic writing, who was shocked by its contents, as shown in a letter to his brother in which he says the following:

"Here, a part of a ritual, in the back of which the human interest had written a sales contract and, there, remains of some images of monstrous obscenity that gave me a really strange impression about Egyptian wisdom and composure. "

The piece itself is configured as a strip of papyrus of 259 cm in length and about 21 cm in height in which two series of very different scenes are depicted, although it appears that the author's idea was to form a unit, a whole whose relationship we don't quite understand yet. The document is now seriously damaged and missing many fragments. Still, the drawings have been almost entirely rebuilt, not least because of conserved tracings made in the nineteenth century, when the papyrus was in much better shape. One of these tracings was made by the Spanish scholar Luis de Usoz, who lived in Turin when the papyrus was purchased, and is now preserved in the National Library in Madrid.

29.- Complete Turin Erotic Papyrus. Above we see the erotic scenes and at the bottom the representation of animals with human attitudes. Reconstruction from copies made in the nineteenth century.

The first part of the document (on the right) shows us a series of drawings of animals, alone or in groups, in fully human styles: a hawk trying to climb up a ladder to a tree where there is a hippo, a lion playing the lyre, a crocodile playing lute, etc. Although we have tried to give these scenes countless interpretations, today we tend to regard them as essentially satirical. This part is very similar in content and style to another papyrus also dating from the Ramesside period and which is now preserved in the British Museum in London.

The part that interests us is also the largest, occupying 170 cm of the total script and is divided into twelve scenes with full sexual content. We see represented several characters having sex in many different positions, most of them almost impossible to implement unless it was with couple of accomplished gymnasts, if not contortionists, and in some of them key characters are accompanied by secondary ones, always drawn in a smaller size. A significant part of the texts that accompanied most of the images have been lost, but they were presented as a dialogue, in a way that remind a comic.

The few texts that have been able to be reconstructed and decoded, in hieratic script, do not unfortunately give us many clues about the meaning of the drawings, as mostly are limited to expressions and dialogues of small size and ambiguous meanings. Although, they are of the most explicit like: "Don't fear what I'm going to do to you," "my God," "put your lovely phallus in me without me seeing it" (i.e., from behind), "do you see it?, the entire phallus has penetrated me. I'm not ashamed," etc. Besides, these texts seem to have been written after the completion of drawings using the space available between scenes, and they may not be contemporary or even come from the same hand.

Much has been discussed about the meaning and function of this papyrus, in fact scholars have not yet agreed on it. For some it is a simple pornographic comic made for the use and enjoyment of a wealthy person of that time; for others however, it narrated the amatory exploits of a particular person—it has even been suggested that he might be Ramses II himself or a priest of Amun, according to some of the elements present. However, it has also been speculated that what is shown is just an orgy or a brothel scene.

The truth is that the male protagonist seems to always be the same, a man advanced in years and balding, with the exception of the scene in which the sexual encounter takes place on a chariot. This could indicate that we have before a story starring a specific person, although it is difficult to assure this one hundred percent due to the poor condition of the papyrus, which does not allow us to safely compare the facial features of the male protagonists.

Some researchers have even raised the possibility that this papyrus is a kind of sexual guide to instruct the men of the Egyptian upper classes, in a similar way in which the *Kama Sutra* was used by Indian nobles, something which we consider unlikely since the Turin papyrus lacks the moral and instructive components of the Indian text.

30.- Detail of the Turin Erotic Papyrus with the first six scenes.

The images: The scenes would be drawn to be seen from right to left, the same way texts were read, so that we have numbered them from 1 to 12 for better identification.

The first image is one showing the woman bent almost in half with the man penetrating her from behind (copulation *a tergo)*. The man has something hanging over his right shoulder which could be a sack, while with his left hand he seems to hit the buttocks of the young woman.

The second scene is one of the most complex, as the man penetrates the woman from behind while she is riding a chariot being pulled by other girls who are incited by a man with an enormous penis. Meanwhile on the chariots' spear a monkey scampers. The man carries a bottle in his right hand and from the same arm hangs a sistrum, while with the other hand he holds the girl by the hair. This detail is repeated in other two scenes.

In the third scene the girl is penetrated while she is sitting on a stool with legs raised. The man raises his hands and looks back as if he were not focused on the action, while she's the one who places his penis between her legs. Under the stool we find the same elements the man was carrying in the previous scene; a bottle and a sistrum, Hathor's instrument.

The fourth scene is one of the most difficult to interpret, since in it the woman appears with open legs facing the viewer, on top of an indeterminate element that some identify as a vessel placed upside down. The tip of the object is right in the vagina of the young woman and the man, who is kneeling beside her, places his finger on it while his huge erect penis almost touches the ground. On the scene there are interpretations for every taste, from those who think that this is a device designed to collect vaginal fluids of the young woman, to those who think that what is drawn is a simple scene of masturbation, which does not seem very logical, since she is also distracted putting on lipstick while looking in a mirror.

In the fifth scene the woman is penetrated while being held in the air by her partner and she lifts her legs over the man's shoulders.

The sixth scene is at the center of the erotic papyrus, and it is also difficult to interpret. The man is lying on the bed while she stretches her arms towards him as if encouraging him to get on the bed, something to which he does not seem very eager. Next to the man we can see both a broken jar and a complete one, which could indicate that the man is drunk.

31.- Detail of the Turin Erotic Papyrus with the last six scenes.

The seventh scene is usually placed in relation to the previous one, because the man is carried in arms by his lover helped by two other women. The man has fainted, and we do not know whether by excess of alcohol or sex. This scene, along with the previous one, are the only ones in where there is no type of sexual contact.

In scene number eight the lovers are in positions reminiscent of representations of the gods Geb and Nut. We see how the man is lying on the floor with his huge erect penis and his hand on his head, just as Geb is often represented, while the woman is arched over him, as Nut, and seems to levitate without the man's penis reaching to penetrate her.

Scene nine again shows us a copulation *a tergo*, and in it the man holds the woman by the hair forcing her to turn her head towards him. This is the most "viable" position of all the ones represented on the papyrus.

Scene ten shows the woman lying on an unspecified surface, with one leg on her partner's shoulder and the other under his armpit. The man penetrates her while seeming to levitate because his feet don't get to touch the ground.

In scene eleven the woman lifts one leg over the man who penetrates her while holding her by the hair. Beside the girl there is a lyre on the floor.

In the twelfth and final scene the man penetrates the woman on top of her, the latter is lying on an incline with one leg over her lover's shoulder, while her hand hangs and is held by a little man, also with an erect penis. Interestingly we found some images of Osiris in which the God is represented in exactly the same position as the young woman.

32.- Detail of scene eleven. The woman lifts one leg over the man who penetrates her while holding her by the hair. Egyptian Museum in Turin.

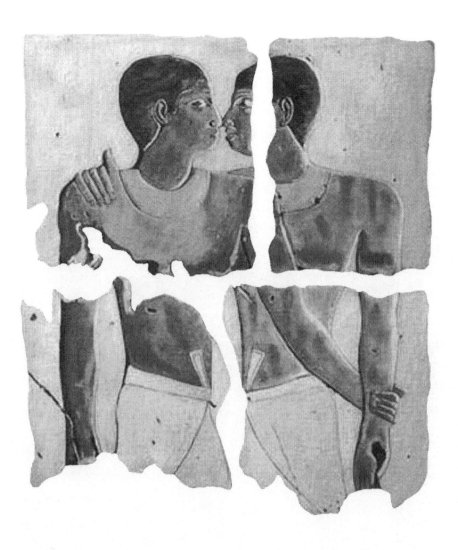

33.- Photograph of one of the scenes painted on the tomb of Khnumhotep and Niankhkhnum in which the couple can be seen in a position clearly of a couple, identical to that shown in numerous graves, but with characters of different gender. Saqqara necropolis.

8.- Homosexuality

While it is clear that homosexuality, both male and female, was present in ancient Egypt the same way as in other ancient and modern societies, the fact is that the express mention in written sources and iconography are more than scarce, so much so that they didn't even have a word to define the relationships between persons of the same sex.

To this original shortage, we must also add the proven fact that until not too many years ago lot of references to sexuality in general (but especially homosexuality) had been hidden, if not directly destroyed.

But shortage doesn't mean absence since we have several references, some extremely important because they allow us to draw critical conclusions about the vision that the ancient Egyptians had of sexual relations between persons of the same sex.

The main one is the story of a legendary episode of the confrontation between the gods Horus and Seth set out in a number of papyri, albeit different versions. One of the longest known, of the early Middle Kingdom (2050-1785 BC), would be summarized as follows: Seth invites Horus to his home and Horus gladly accepts the invitation. In the evening both lie in the same bed and during the night Seth places his erect penis between the thighs of Horus. Horus collected Seth's semen and went to see his mother Isis asking for her help, Isis cut off Horus' hand and the hand full of semen fell into the Nile. Then Horus masturbated, his mother took the semen and placed it on a lettuce which was consumed by Seth. Later, when Seth boasted to the Ennead (nine major gods of the Heliopolitan cosmogony) that he had done the work of a "warrior man" in Horus, i.e., that he had penetrated him, Horus fought back saying otherwise, that it had been him the one who had acted as a "warrior man" on Seth. Then the Ennead cried aloud to the semen of Seth to see where it had fertilized, and immediately the bamboo and papyrus from the banks of the Nile answered, and when they called to the semen of Horus to see where it had been fertilized, Seth threw up Horus' semen which he had swallowed with lettuce.

An older version tells the same story but in a slightly different and more explicit version:

"The divine person of Seth told the divine person of Horus: 'How beautiful are your buttocks, how vital'...'Open your legs'...Then (Horus) ran and told her mother Isis that Seth wanted to sodomize him...And she said, 'Watch out! Do not get too close to him! When he mentions it again, then you will say:

It's very painful for me' ... "I beg you not to push your strength in me" ... Isis continued her advice: 'Then when he pushes with his strength, place your fingers between your buttocks.'...'Behold, he will enjoy to the fullest of that seed that has come out'...Later, Isis threw Seth's semen in a nearby stream, then he spread some of Horus' semen in a lettuce and gave it to Seth to eat. Later, when Seth boasted to the gods that he had sexually taken Horus, the young man denied it. To settle the argument, the gods called out the seeds of both. Seth's seed answered from the water...While the seed of Horus came out of Seth's forehead in the shape of a golden disc."

(Montserrat, 1996, 141)

Regardless of what this myth in its various versions tries to convey in relation to the struggles between the Upper and Lower Egypt (Seth was the god of Upper Egypt and Horus of Lower Egypt), who ended up uniting under a single crown, we see how they all emphasize the persistence of both contenders to show that it was they who had exercised the active role in bed. None deny that such sexual encounters occurred, but both seek to demonstrate that it is the other who was sodomized, implying submission as an important role. Moreover, this attitude toward male homosexuality is common to other nearby cultures such as the Phoenicians and Mesopotamians.

We must not forget that some contemporary sources considered Seth to be effeminate, for example in an inscription of the temple of Edfu they refer to Seth as "that who is like a woman" (*hemety*).

A second reference to male homosexuality, gathered by at least three different papyri, is the one that tells of the night meetings of Pharaoh Neferkare (Pepi II, of the VI Dynasty) with General Sasenet. The story, as a tale, tells how a man named Teti on one night saw the Pharaoh leave the palace alone and decided to follow him, as there were rumors about the monarch's nights out. When Pepi came to general Sasenet's house he threw a stone and they immediately threw a ladder by which he entered the house, where he remained for four hours allegedly cavorting with his general.

A noteworthy aspect is that, as in the episode of Seth and Horus, these papyri do not try to morally assess the homosexual act itself, but are rather critical against the pharaoh for what they consider an abuse of power over his commander. Although it could also be argued that nowhere it is said that the General disagreed with such samples of royal affection nor specified safely which one exercised the role of "warrior man" and which one was the submissive one, something that as we have seen previously, was a detail of the utmost importance to the Egyptian mentality. I dread to think what would have happened if word had been spread that it was the pharaoh himself, god on earth, who had allowed himself to be sodomized by Sasenet.

It has also been speculated that the references to act as a "warrior man" come from possible violations practiced upon those vanquished in the battlefield as a way to humiliate them.

34.- Another copy of the scenes painted on the tomb of Khnumhotep and Niankhkhnum in which the two men appear cuddling and their faces close together, in a very different way from how men are represented in Egyptian art.

Another case of possible male homosexuality can be found in a tomb discovered in Saqqara in 1964 and dating from the reign of Pharaoh Niuserre (2453-2422 B.C.). This is known as the "tomb of the two brothers," a tomb housing the remains of two men who held the post of royal manicurists and chief manicurists of the palace, and that initially were considered to be twins (Khnumhotep and Niankhkhnum). But it seems increasingly clear that there was a relationship between both that had nothing to do with brotherly love. For starters, over the entrance to the inner chambers we find their names intertwined—Niankh-Jnum-Hotep—so that they could be read as "bound together in life and in death," and the most striking thing is that in the interior walls they are represented in various scenes in caring attitudes unknown in Egyptian art between two men: embracing, holding hands or joining their noses into what looks like the prelude to a kiss. Although in these scenes they are surrounded by their wives and children, most researchers believe that what we are really seeing is the first representation of a homosexual couple in art history. If we follow the usual conventions in Egyptian art, in this relationship Khnumhotep would be the one whom would exercise the female function, and so we see him hugging Niankhkhnum, who in turn leads Khumhotep by the hand.

Apart from these most striking cases, we find several references to relations of the homoerotic kind in various texts, among which stand out the Coffin Texts and the Book of the Dead.

The following passage appears in the formula 635 of the Coffin Texts: "Atum has no power over (name of the deceased), he copulated with his anus." We believe that this formula is not directly related to homosexuality, but refers to the relationship of power that is attributed to sodomizing another man. By penetrating another individual, even Atum himself is deprived of his powers over the deceased.

The Book of the Dead is an ancient collection of spells, prayers and other funerary texts that began to be written from the XVIII Dynasty, and a copy of it used to be placed in the coffins of the deceased, although each one gathered different passages.

Chapter 125, known as the "negative confession" includes two series of confessions that the deceased makes before the Heavenly Court, presided over by Osiris, to try to convince them that one is worthy of eternal life. These statements are some that proves the existence of homosexual relationships. For example one of these confessions has been translated as "I have not had sex with a child" as well as "I have not copulated with a penetrated one" and "I did not sexually penetrate another man." Different interpretations are due to the different ways of translating the word *nkk*. Despite the nuances, all these forms expressly refer to a relationship of a homosexual nature.

In the Prisse papyrus preserved in the National Library in Paris, which includes "The Teachings of the Vizier Ptahhotep," a compendium of moral precepts, we find the passage 32 which indicates that it is inappropriate to copulate with a "woman-boy," a term which could be translated as a boy or young person who would correspond to a passive role in a homosexual relationship, which would be an indication that it was not uncommon to use children as sex objects.

Egyptologist Richard B. Parkinson also cites an inscription in the temple of Edfu (Memphis) and in a papyrus from Tanis in the Delta, which indicate that it is taboo to "join with an *hm* (an effeminate man) or with a *nkk* (passive homosexual)".

Another thing that changed with the arrival of the Greeks in Egypt was the view of homosexuality, as everyone knows that sex between men was a common and socially accepted practice throughout the Greek cultural sphere.

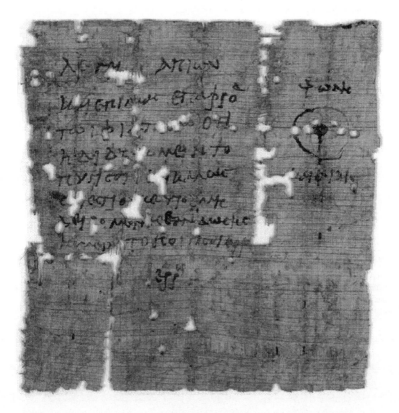

35.- Papyrus letter located in Oxyrhynchus with a clear homosexual content. The drawing supposedly represents an anus being penetrated. It is dated in the first century B.C. Ashmolean Museum, Oxford.

One of the best known records to come to us from that time is the one found contained in a letter on papyrus located in 1897 on a former Oxyrhynchus landfill (now El-Bahnasa) by archaeologists Bernard P. Grenfell and Arthur S. Hunt, which is deposited in the Ashmolean Museum of Oxford University. It is dated from the first century B.C. and it reads:

"Apion and Epimas proclaim to Epaphroditos, the best beloved, that if you allow us to sodomize you, it will go well for you, and we will not thrash you any longer if you allow us to sodomize. Farewell."(P. Oxy. 3070 XLII)

In addition to the message, the letter includes a drawing, albeit of very limited artistic quality, but it is most eloquent: a hole with something like a stick penetrating it. In addition they added the text: at the top they wrote what could be translated as "hard-on" and at the bottom "and ass." Unfortunately we haven't found an answer to the letter, so we are left to wonder what happened to Epaphroditos.

Already during Roman domination we find an event of great importance for the subject under discussion, the death of Antinous, the young lover of Emperor Hadrian, drowned in the Nile. The emperor never got over it, and devoted much effort and money to perpetuate the memory of the young man: minted coins with his effigy, founded the city of Antinoopolis in the place where he died and even made a cult to him associated with Osiris.

These circumstances have revealed to us another case of homosexuality among Egyptians, but, as we say, it was from a very late period. In that same city of Antinoopolis, archaeologists found in the late nineteenth century a double funerary portrait, dating from the second century AD, depicting two men—one much younger than the other—and that at the beginning, again, they had been considered to be brothers. Similar to the other tale of the brothers, there are many who argue that their relationship was far from fraternal, suggesting instead that they were a homosexual couple who decided to share their existence also in the hereafter.

Several factors contribute to this change of interpretation; one is the new perspective when observing the relationships in the past, also the zero existing resemblance between the two men, the fact that the youngest was painted with clear skin, as it used to be with women and, very importantly, the presence of an image of Antinoosiris, Hadrian's deified lover, just above the shoulder of the youngest partner.

Similarly as we find cases of sexual violence against women, there has been found at least one court case concerning a possible violation of a homosexual type:

"Charges concerning the violation by this sailor Panetta (...), a farmer of Knum temple, Lord of Elephantine, who is in the city of Pa (...)" (Turin Papyrus 1887, v°3, 4-5)

We insist here on the fact that for Egyptians, male anal penetration was above all an act of domination and humiliation on the person performing the passive role, something more obvious when, as in this case, the relationship was nonconsensual.

If few are the references to male homosexuality, lesbian relations are almost nonexistent, since they are limited to three texts. The first is contained in the papyrus Carlsberg XIII, a book of dream interpretation dating from the second century B.C.:

"If a woman has sex with her, she will have bad luck, and one of

Sex and Erotism in Ancient Egypt

his sons (...); if a woman has sex with her, she will lie."
Manniche, L. (1987)

The fact that these lesbian sex relations are mentioned (although these might occur within a dream), suggests it was something known, but what we don't know is whether these would be frequent and the degree of social acceptance.

The second reference is less clear, since it appears in a passage from the Book of the Dead on Nestanebtasheru papyrus (970 B.C.), which reads that "She has never had sex with the wife of a man." We don't know whether or not the scribe meant this or simply made a mistake when copying the text from a male, since this is a unique case and, as these books usually have almost standardized formulas, it is very rare for this passage not to appear in any other papyrus among many located in female graves.

We find one last reference to these lesbian tendencies in a spell that has come down to us in which a woman asks the gods of the afterlife to intercede to make another woman fall in love with her, indicating even the place where the love affair between the two women should take place: a bathhouse. But we must remember that we are talking about the Ptolemaic period and that the characters have Greek names, with which is difficult to extrapolate this episode to earlier times:

"(...) Through this spirit of dead ignite the heart, the liver, the spirit of Gorgonia, who was born of Nilogenia, and ignite her with love and desire towards Sofia, who was born of Isara.

Force Gorgonia, who was born of Nilogenia, to go to the baths, for Sofia, who was born of Isara. And you, Send her to the baths. Burn, ignite, arouse her soul, her heart, her liver, her spirit, of love for Sophia, who was born of Isara.

Bring me Gorgonia, who was born of Nilogenia. Attract her to me, torture her body night and day, subdue her, to abruptly leave every place and every house for the love of Sophia, who was born of Isara, to be delivered to her as a slave, giving her all of her belongings as well(...) ". (SGD 151. Hermopolis)

After studying all these sources, perhaps the most important aspect that emerges from it is that the "official" position was to consider homosexuality as a reprehensible conduct to be avoided, especially because it was not productive in terms of begetting offspring, a point as we saw above, was of great importance in the Egyptian mentality. But there would be no specific legal prohibition. This lack of prohibition would be reflected in the fact that there's no known sentence for practicing sodomy, which does occur in other ancient cultures. But we must not forget that the fact that it appears in the confessions of the Book of the Dead as one of the actions that the deceased must claim to not have performed in his life tells us that homosexual relations were among the activities to avoid if a person wanted to access the afterlife.

On the other hand, it doesn't seem that the general public saw these relationships as something strange and degenerated, but it appears to be a socially accepted practice.

36.- Figure of a nude man standing who has an erection. Ivory sculpture. Naqada period (late predynastic period). Louvre Museum in Paris.

37.- Known *ostracon* depicting a topless dancer in action. Some researchers believe that some of these dancers would also be prostitutes, who in addition to exhibiting their dances would sell their bodies. Possibly proceeding from Deir el-Medina. Egyptian Museum in Turin.

9.- Prostitution

Prostitution existed in ancient Egypt just as it existed in the vast majority of cultures of the ancient Mediterranean, and that is something that has been reflected in several sources, mainly written.

One of the best known references to prostitution in the country of the Nile brings us to the Greek historian Herodotus, who lived in the 5th century BC, and that tells us that the Pharaoh Khufu (26th century BC), in need of money to finish his pyramid, forced one of his daughters to work in a brothel until she got a certain sum.

Obviously this is a crude attempt of attack on the figure of the king whom Herodotus was not too fond of, because he considered him a tyrant and a criminal. But the fact that he mentions this activity indicates that it was a real practice, known at that time. Let's remember, this is before the Greek conquest. Indeed, it appears that the daughter of Cheops discovered how profitable that business was or really liked it, because according to Herodotus the girl continued to work in the brothel after having collected the amount requested by her father, but from that moment on she earned it for herself, as she required each of her customers to pay a stone for her own tomb. According to the Greek historian, with this activity the girl would have built the central pyramid of the three next to Cheops'.

More than a few researchers believe that the famous Turin Papyrus shows scenes developed inside a brothel, or at least the protagonist would be a prostitute, given the undeniable hability of the woman or women represented in the drawings, pointing to a professional in the sector.

Some scholars believe that the images depicted in some scenes where women are portrayed with tattoos of the god Bes on their thighs would actually correspond to prostitutes, as well.

We also find some texts where it prevents men from seeking the company of prostitutes, such as papyrus 10508 from the British Museum, of the late period, which reflects the instruction of Ankhsheshonq, and tells us the following:

"He who makes love to a hooker will have his moneybag cut and open on one side"

Another important subject of note is that of so-called sacred prostitution. Much has been said of the possible existence of sacred prostitution in Egyptian temples, but the truth is that there is no clear and obvious proof thereof, indeed, the ancient authors contradict each other.

On the one hand Strabo (64 B.C.-21 A.D.) mentions the practice of prostitution in the Temple of Amun:

"They devoted to Zeus (Amun) one of the most beautiful girls and from the most illustrious family ... she would become a prostitute and had relations with anyone who ask her until the purification of her body would take place (until she had her first menstruation)".

But on the other hand we also have the words of Herodotus, who tells us that among the things that attracted his attention about the Egyptians was the fact that they banned having sex in temples, which would indicate that sacred prostitution was prohibited as it was normally practiced within the sacred precincts.

In the same line is found what is gathered in the Book of the Dead. Among one of those "negative confessions" the dead says "I have not had relations with a woman in the holy places of the god of my city."

This apparent contradiction between Strabo and Herodotus might not be of such significance, because we must not forget that between these two authors there were four centuries of difference, and that the time of Strabo was about the change of era, and Egypt was a Roman province with many customs that would have been changed to adapt to their new masters.

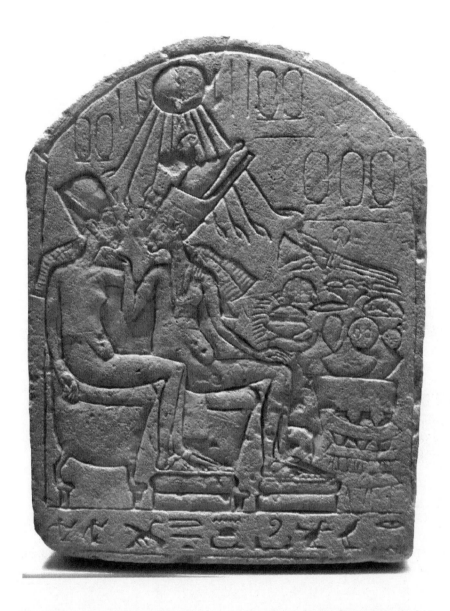

38.- Stele representing Akhenaten and his wife Nefertiti (XVIII Dynasty). In this relief we can see the delicate signs of affection that the king dedicated to his wife, a typical art detail from Amarna period, far from the rigid official aesthetic of the rest of Egyptian history. Berlin Museum.

10.- Erotic Poetry

Egyptian erotic/romantic poetry is extremely important for today's researchers, because it allows us to have a firsthand view of what intimate relationships were like more than three thousand years ago, and what the feelings were like for those men and women who were yearning to be together to enjoy their love, the same as any today's couple. Something that has caught the attention of researchers is the freshness and modernity of these poems, which flourished especially in Ramesside times (approx. 1291 to 1069 BC).

Although some of them refer to married couples, they usually seem to refer to romantic relations between teen couples, because it is frequently mentioned that the lovers live in separate houses, something illogical if they were married.

These literary works are known in the West since the late nineteenth century and are included in almost thirty papyri and *ostraca*, containing about 80 poems or songs, and it seems clear that at least some of these texts have been composed to be sung, not recited.

The vast majority of known poems come from the settlement of Deir el-Medina, the village of the builders of the tombs in the Valley of the Kings.

The content and tone can range from the most platonic and romantic love to direct sexual desire, and the authors thereof may be either male or female. There are not many differences in how each gender addresses this issue, both show openly the desire to be next to each other and in many cases sexual references are openly discussed. Some authors point out that those told from a female point of view are more direct than those narrated by men.

There are examples that grab our attention by the original way to address de issue, as this one from an ostracon which is kept at the French Institute of Oriental Archaeology in Cairo:

"When I kiss her and her lips are open,
I'm drunk even without drinking beer."
(Cairo *Ostracon* 25218, 15-16)

In the following example a woman clearly arouses the desire of her beloved:

"I come with you, my god, my husband.
It's delicious to go down the river
and do what you ask me:
entering the water, bathing in-front of you.

I let you see my beauty

under the thin linen tunic,

soaked in essences,

impregnated with oils.

To be with you

I immerse myself in the river and come out

with a red fish in hands.

He is happy in my fingers.

I put it on my breasts.

Oh my god, my husband

come and look.". (Deir el-Medina *Ostracon* 1266. Manniche)

In this next poem it is a man who is the one who shows total devotion to his beloved, to whom he wants to be with at all times, even wanting to be her sandals to be trodden by her feet. Today this love would be considered a clear example of fetishism, or even a lover of domination:

"I wish I were your mirror

so that you always looked at me.

I wish I were your garment

so that you would always wear me.

I wish I were the water

that washes your body.

I wish I were the unguent,

O Woman,

that I could anoint you.

And the band around your breasts,

and the beads around your neck.

I wish I were your sandal

that you would step on me! (Papyrus Anakreon.)

Below, another sign of love and dedication from a lover:

"Sister without rival,

most beautiful of all,

she looks like the goddess rising star

at the start of a good New Year.

Perfect and bright, shining skin,

seductive in her eyes when she glances,

sweet in her lips when she speaks,

and never a word too many." (Papyrus Chester Beatty I, Dublin)

In the Harris 500 Papyrus we find another poem starring a woman who has no problem showing complete sexual desire for her beloved:

"If ever, my dear, I should not be here,

where would you offer your heart?

If I could not hold you by my side,

How would you know again the satisfaction of love?

Would your fingers follow the lines of my thighs, would they know

the curves of my breasts, and the rest?

It's all here, love quickly discovered (...)

Here, place my breast next to you.

Yours, my offering full as the love I give you,

overflowing, with no end (...)

How splendid is a full day made pure by love
(Being in contact face to face)!
My heart is not yet sated to make love to you,
my (small) wolf cub!

As we see, these poems have full force and could have been written today by any lover or current poet, showing us how little we have changed in our romantic feelings and how to express them, despite the intervening millennia.

39.- Fragment of a painted relief from Ptolemaic era depicting a couple copulating with both lovers lying sideways. (New York) Brooklyn Museum.

11.- Conclusion

As we have seen, the reality we're reading about differs largely from the stereotypes that most people have about what sexuality would be like among the ancient Egyptians. The sensuality transmitted to us by many of their images, with women who are nude or covered by just a few transparencies are not accompanied with explicit sex scenes. The explicit scenes we find are more often relegated only to the world of the gods.

However, it is also true that samples of erotic art would originally be much more abundant, that papyri such as Turin's wouldn't necessarily be a rarity among Egyptians from their respective eras, and in monuments there were likely hundreds of depictions of ithyphallic gods, but the ignorance and inflexibility of those whom were supposed to curate and protect such ancient images instead decided it was obscene and degenerate, undeserving to subsist to posterity, so the ancient art was destroyed.

Yet we shouldn't lose hope in locating new pieces of erotic art in excavations that continue to happen throughout Egypt, and it is also quite possible that works that once went directly to private collections because their discoverers or, more often the authorities of that time, decided these were not suitable pieces to be displayed in serious museums, will reappear again. This is something that can be easily checked by simply taking a look at the catalogs of the most prestigious auction houses, where it isn't uncommon to find these pieces, especially from the Ptolemaic era (and that reach very high prices by the way).

Surely there are also many pieces that are still slumbering in their sleep of centuries in boxes covered with dust, forgotten for decades in the last corners of museum warehouses, hoping that one day someone will rescue them and return them to the places they belong: in the broad daylight in public displays, where all aspects of human life must be displayed, and where art as important as this deserves to be recognized.

That is why I am convinced that knowledge of the world of sex and eroticism among the ancient Egyptians will not stop increasing with new pieces and new studies from researchers who today are working to shed new light on one the most interesting and least known aspects of the fascinating civilization of the children of the Nile.

Dear reader, I want to spend my last few lines to thank you for choosing my book and for reaching the end of its reading, which hopefully means that you liked it. If so, I would ask you to dedicate one minute to review it at Amazon to help other readers find what they seek.

Best regards, I hope we meet again in my next work.

http:// benjamincollado.com

Bibliography

- Baines, J. y Málek, J. Egipto. Dioses, templos y faraones. Folio, Madrid. 1992.

- Brewer, D.J. y Teeter, E. Egypt and the Egyptians. Cambridge University Press, 2001.

- Leaspo, E. y Tosi, M. La donna nell'antico Egitto. Giunti, 1997

- Manniche L. Sexual Life in Ancient Egypt. KPI, London/New York. 1987

- Meskell, L. Private Life in New Kingdom Egypt. Princeton University Press. Princeton. 2002.

- Montserrat, D. Sex and Society in Graeco-Roman Egypt. Kegan Paul, London and New York. 1996.

- O'Connor, D. "Eros in Egypt", Archaeology Odyssey, 5, pp.42-51. 2001

- Omlin J. Der Papyrus 55001 und seine satirisch-erotischen Zeichnungen und Inschriften Turin 21. Berlin Akademic Verlag: Berlin.1973.

- Orriols, M. "Léxico e iconografía erótica del antiguo Egipto. El coito a tergo", Trabajos de Egiptología, 5/2, pp. 123-137. 2009.

- Orriols, M. "Mujer ideal, mujer infractora. La trasgresión femenina en el Antiguo Egipto". Lectora, 18, pp. 17-40. 2012.

- Parra, J.M. "La violencia doméstica en el Egipto Antiguo".

Trabajos de Egiptología, 5-2. 2009.

- Parra, J.M. Vida amorosa en el antiguo Egipto. Sexo, matrimonio y erotismo. Aldebarán, Madrid. 2001.

- Reeder, Greg. "Same-Sex Desire, Conyugal Constructs, and the tomb of Niankhkhnum and Khnumhotep", World Archaeology, 32/2, Oct. 2000, p. 193-208.

- Schmidt, R.A. y Voss, B. (eds). Archaeologies of Sexuality. Routledge. London and New York. 2000.

- Shokeir, A.A. y Hussein, M.I. "Sexual Life in Pharaonic Egypt: Towards a Urological View". International Journal of Impotence Research. 16, pp. 385-388. 2004.

- Stead, M. La vida en el Antiguo Egipto. Akal, 1998.

- Strouhal, E. La vida en el Antiguo Egipto. Folio, 2005.

- Sweeney, D. "Gender and Language in the Ramesside Love Songs". BES, 16, pp. 27-50. 2002.

- Toivari-Viitala, J. Women at Deir el Medina. A Study of the Status and Roles of the Female Inhabitants in the Workmen's Community during the Ramesside Period (EgyptologischeUitgaven 15), Leiden, NeerlansInstituutvoor het nabijeoosten.

Images Credits:

Michael Horn: 0; London British Museum: 1, 4 down, 5, 19 and 26; Laura Parker: 2; Louvre Museum:7, 20, 36; Henry Walters: 8;

Iovani Russo: 9; Lisa Watson: 14; *Yorck Project:16;* Ismail Yazar: 21; Lasse Jensen:22; Antonio Luci: 32; Justin Howard: 34;Yasir Mushtaq: 33; Marisa Levoni: 37; Ferdinand Mamoulian: 38.

18884641R00076

Printed in Poland
by Amazon Fulfillment
Poland Sp. z o.o., Wrocław